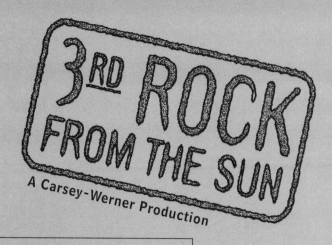

3RD ROCK FROM THE SUN

A Carsey-Werner Production

SUBJECT

The Official Report on Earth

NAME

High Commander Dick Solomon

By the creators and writers of 3rd Rock from the Sun

MICHAEL GLOUBERMAN

BOB KUSHELL

BILL MARTIN

ANDREW ORENSTEIN

DAVID SACKS

MIKE SCHIFF

BONNIE TURNER

TERRY TURNER

CHRISTINE ZANDER

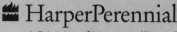 HarperPerennial

A Division of HarperCollinsPublishers

To The Humans

FIRST EDITION

Designed by Joel Avirom, Jason Snyder, and Meghan Day Healey

ISBN 0-06-095228-8

96 97 98 99 00 ❖ 10 9 8 7 6 5 4 3

CONTENTS

ll

or-

ow
he
ky
s

began
small
accu-
Moon,
ve been
ed. In
o the
and-
s mis-

s not
ok"

ontent
mind
ation
ur

To: Big Giant Head
From: High Commander (aka Professor Dick Solomon)
Re: Planet Earth

We have been here on Earth for nearly what the humans call "a year." You have requested a report on the "Third Rock from the Sun." I do not feel we have compiled enough information. However, since your word is supreme law, we are forwarding our report to be used by those who would follow us to study this obscure planet located in an outpost of the galaxy the humans have affectionately nicknamed the "Milky Way" (after a popular candy bar). I hope you will find it helpful. I wish someone had done it for us. This place is not exactly what we expected.

As you remember, it wasn't long ago that we first began to hear the radio waves that were emitting from this small blue dot. Much of the information we received was inaccurate. For example, the oft repeated command "To the Moon, Alice!" has nothing to do with space travel. They have been to the Moon, but there was no one named Alice involved. In fact, as it turns out, no women were allowed to go to the Moon at all. Sally, our second in command, is understandably upset since she agreed to be "the woman" on this mission based on the "Alice Directives."

Other things you should know: "Yabba Dabba Doo" is not a code for anything. The man who said "I am not a crook" was. But we were right on one thing—Madonna is a slut.

We are at times confused, but we remain alert and patient. Other than Sally's frustration, we are all content with our mission. I am fine in my human body. I don't mind having to be the tall dashing man of the unit. Information officer Tommy is glad to be an adolescent, and Harry, our receiver/transmitter, is just glad to be anywhere.

← My human form.
Quite handsome, I must say.

INTRODUCTION

In March of 1994, in a restaurant in Los Angeles, California, I was abducted by aliens. They had taken the form of television producers and comedy writers. They called themselves "The Carsey-Werner Company."

Looking back on the event, I marvel at how easily I was taken in. The aliens had shrewdly arranged the meeting through my agent, instructing him to inform me that my "old friends Bonnie and Terry" wanted to have breakfast with me. And that they wanted me to meet some new friends — Tom, Marcy, and Caryn. As I joined them at their table in the plush confines of the Four Seasons hotel, they seemed harmless enough: benign, chucklesome, intelligent, almost human.

Having researched the typical profile of the earthling actor, they knew my vulnerability to the blandishments of writer-producers. So they set about to use a subtle, insidious weapon on me: the television situation-comedy pitch.

Situation comedy. Sitcom! The very word had always sounded faintly cheesy to me. From my early days as an idealistic young actor, I had left only one rule unbroken: Never do a sitcom. And as they launched into their pitch, my resolve was utterly intact. I smiled indulgently. I may even have imperceptibly shaken my head and rolled my eyes as I silently rehearsed the phrases I would use to turn them down.

"It's about four aliens," Terry began.

"Yeah, right," I inwardly replied.

What a fool I was! What a pathetically deluded fool! Did I catch no whiff of the paranormal? Spot no hint of the extraterrestrial? Did nothing about these people strike me as even a little . . . well, strange?

How fiendishly clever of them to hide in plain sight! It was a sitcom about them!

As the pitch continued, they deployed another weapon from their alien arsenal: they made me laugh. They told me about Sally, the fearless warrior back home who, here on Earth, had been forced to accept the ignominious role of "the woman." They told me about Tommy, the world-weary elder back home, trapped in the earthly body of an adolescent boy percolating with hormones. They told me about Harry, the dull tool, a dimwit back home and a dimwit here too, whose role on the mission was that of a simple transmitter, a conduit to their other world. Best of all, they told me about Dick Solomon, the high commander. Imperious, impetuous, romantic, myopic, and innocent, Dick was a role for Jacques Tati, for John Cleese, for Groucho, for Chaplin, for Benny, for *me*. The role of Dick was the Turners' most potent weapon of all. They unleashed it on me and I was a goner.

Abducted! That was over two years ago, and I have been in captivity ever since. Nor am I alone. Their spacecraft resembles a soundstage in Studio City, California, and it is manned by a much larger crew of aliens who are billeted nearby in Writers' Building #2. Their diabolical scheme is to change the way the human race views itself, and alas, I have become their confederate. If you find this note . . . help me! Please!

—John Lithgow

High Commander's Note:
I have no idea who this John Lithgow fellow is, or what this story is doing here. Tommy, my information officer, says that Lithgow is an Earth actor who was in some helicopter movie. Well la-de-da.

1 Welcome to Earth

he beje-

light.

uch

SO, YOU'RE VISITING EARTH ...

Earth is here.

There are several things you will need to know about this interesting and exciting planet.

HOW TO GET THERE

Exit our system at the Alpha 324 arm of the barred spiral on the Cetheus-Draco border. Travel in the trailing direction of the "Big Bang." Continue until you are one light-year from the "Black Wall." (Note: This is important! Do *not* mention the concept of the "Black Wall" on Earth. Humans believe that the Universe goes on forever— they have not yet discovered that it is in a box. The "Black Wall" will only scare them.) Once you see the "Black Wall," turn left and follow the noise until you come to a rather nondescript yellow star. Count out three and there you are: Earth, the third rock.

PLANET TYPE

The Earth is a class-9 blue planet. It has a hard outer crust and a wonderful molten, chewy center.

NATIVE LIFE FORMS

When you arrive, you will be delighted to find the Earth populated with intelligent life. These marvelous creatures are abundant and distributed throughout the planet. They are clever, dependable, loving, and can quickly learn simple tasks. All they ask for is a pat on the head.

Unfortunately, dogs are not in charge. Humans are.

Humans are primitive, carbon-based life-forms. They have mastered radio communications, nuclear fusion, and rocket propulsion. They have even built a "smart bomb" so accurate it can pinpoint a target the size of a postage stamp. But when it snows, they have to close the airport.

LANDING SITES

As you have heard, there allegedly is a rule on Earth that goes, "Aliens land in cornfields." But, be warned—

YOU MUST AVOID CORNFIELDS! We cannot stress this enough. Every local yahoo is always lurking about in the cornfields ready to capture you, shoot you in the head, or just scare the bejesus out of you with a flash camera.

The best landing sites are among large crowds in broad daylight.

Las Vegas: Arrive with all the ship's lights on. Make as much noise as possible. You may even get work.

Any event that ends with the words "pride parade"
Hundreds of spectators will thank you for your support, and the local authorities do not want trouble.

NFL football game parking lots: You'll fit right in with the people in weird costumes, most of whom behave in a barely human manner. If the authorities notice you landing, they will assume you are breaking in and order you to leave. At which point you will drive out among the unsuspecting traffic.

Major cities during rush hour: No one will panic. More than likely they will be annoyed. Humans love to blow the horn and extend one of their long bony fingers. This means, "Welcome! And keep moving." The ideal place of this type: midtown Manhattan.

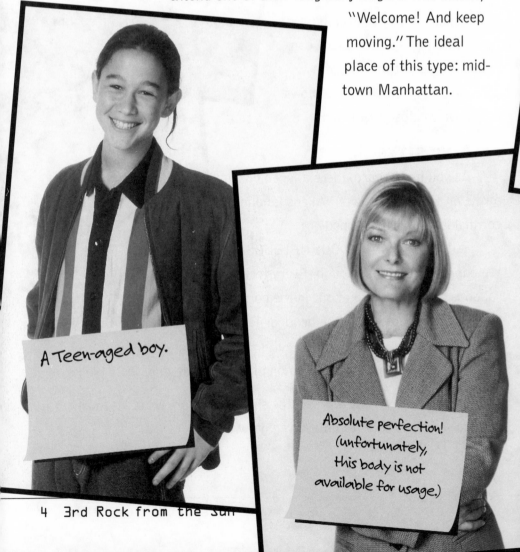

A Teen-aged boy.

Absolute perfection! (unfortunately, this body is not available for usage.)

SO MANY DIFFERENT TYPES OF HUMANS

It's time to decide what you will look like. A gelatinous purple tube will not serve you well on Earth, so . . .

LET'S PICK A HUMAN BODY TYPE

When you arrive, you should notice that there are a variety of humans on the Earth. At first you may think, "So what, they all look alike to me," but believe me, humans can tell the difference. You will have to learn to do the same.

Humans make many distinctions between people. It fills up conversation and helps them identify each other. Remember this when deciding what type you will morph into. You will be expected to accurately describe yourself to people—unless you are having phone sex, and then all bets are off. (Phones, sex, and bets will be explained later.)

At first, choosing a human persona will seem challenging, but the chart opposite contains a series of nouns and adjectives that will help you. Mix and match to describe the people around you.

Let's try and describe a human. Look in the crowd and spot someone. Now go to the chart and check all those that apply. Guess what? That "new human friend" at the Pepsi machine is a "loud, sweaty, beady-eyed, white man with a thick neck and a gut."

Now you combine nouns and adjectives in your mind and try to picture the kind of human you would like to be. Say, "an athletic young Asian woman with pert breasts and fiery eyes." That's a nice picture. Certainly nicer than the large sweaty fat guy. In fact, if I looked like the young Asian woman, I'd be home having sex with myself right now! Haha. That was a "joke," but more on humor later.

Above all, don't be afraid to be what you like. The truly great thing about the human race is that, despite all of their differences, everyone on the planet is equal . . . except when it comes to sex, race, color, creed, national origin, age, height, weight, physical impairments, hair color, intelligence, muscularity, breast size, odor, speech pattern, education, wealth, charisma, breeding, manner, tendency to sweat, and looks. These are the *only* exceptions.

Sex	Age	Body Type	Race/National Origin/Creed	Description	Body Parts
			white	pert	navel
male	young	trim	Asian	sagging	legs
female	old	fat	Filipino	sweaty	arms
boy	middle-aged	fit	Hispanic	shopworn	breasts
girl	teen	firm	Samoan	good-looking	feet
man	child	muscular	English	swarthy	hands
woman	twenty-five	dumpy	Canadian	dreamy	buttocks
babe	boomer	tall	Catholic	godlike	eyes
hunk	ancient	short	Protestant	sweet	gut
goddess	legal	doughy	Jewish	vicious	knees
troll	thirtysomething	shapely	Hindu	loud	neck
harpy	generation X	lithe	African-American	hot	ankles
stud	worn	skinny	Aboriginal	vapid	thighs
guy	fresh	huge	Presbyterian	reptilian	tongue
grandma	tired	bearlike	Celtic	cheap	teeth
gramps	retired	gelatinous	Floridian	stinky	nose
kid	toddler	tiny	New Zealander	beady-eyed	hair
mother	crone	thick	punk	fiery	toes
father	infant	athletic			

ANATOMICAL CHART

The following is an anatomical chart of the human body. I've pointed
out areas of interest that correspond to every single human in the world.
The only thing that may be different are their hats.

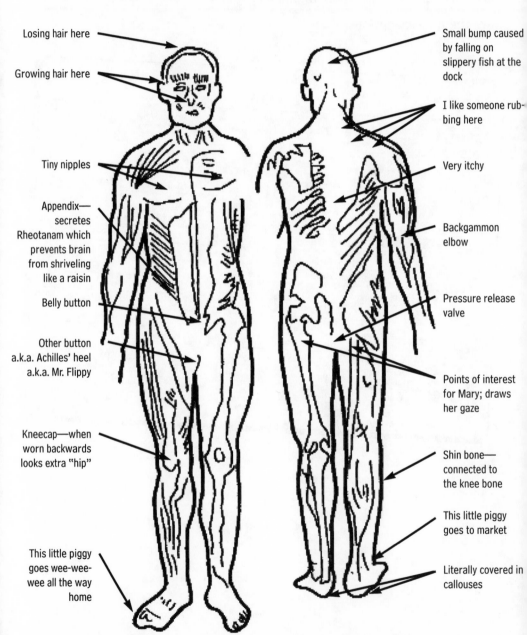

Losing hair here

Growing hair here

Tiny nipples

Appendix—
secretes
Rheotanam which
prevents brain
from shriveling
like a raisin

Belly button

Other button
a.k.a. Achilles' heel
a.k.a. Mr. Flippy

Kneecap—when
worn backwards
looks extra "hip"

This little piggy
goes wee-wee-
wee all the way
home

Small bump caused
by falling on
slippery fish at the
dock

I like someone rub-
bing here

Very itchy

Backgammon
elbow

Pressure release
valve

Points of interest
for Mary; draws
her gaze

Shin bone—
connected to
the knee bone

This little piggy
goes to market

Literally covered in
callouses

A WARNING FROM TOMMY, THE INFORMATION OFFICER, ON BODY TYPE

Regardless of what anybody might tell you, always come to this planet as a fully grown man. To carry out your mission in the body of a fifteen-year-old is hell on Earth. You can't drive, you can't wreck your health with cigarettes, and you can't see NC-17 movies.

I swear, if it weren't for Lisa, Cheryl, August, Dina, Laurie, Alison, Cherie, Liz, Stephanie, Heather, Jennifer, Jessica, Jackie, Kathy, Amy, Beth, Becky, Christine, Kathy, Flora, Carrie, Rachel, Joan, Kelly, Lisa, Judy, Nancy, Monica, Michelle, Stacey, Tammy, Shauna, Miriam, Randie, Sharon, Ann, Marcy, Karen, Susan, Joanne, Jane, Cindy, Bonnie, Sylvia, Sarah, Louise, Robin, Mindy, Mandy, Donna, Marsha, Amber, Celeste, Helen, Ashley, Marilyn, Emily, Kimberly, Tina, Naomi, Natalie, Melanie, Denise, Shelly, Valerie, Daniella, Jody, Audrey, Melissa, Lucy, Julie, Elise, Cynthia, Jill, Joyce, Linda, Molly, Sandy, Donna, Vicki, Alice, Paula, Paige, Jeannie, Leah, Carolyn, Sonya, the cashier at the Quick Mart, Mrs. Talbot, the babe in the red tube top in the AC/DC video, all the "Baywatch" girls, the UPS driver, the girl who works Wednesdays and Saturdays at Weenie-On-A-Stick, the one who works Thursdays and Sundays, Madonna just up to "Like a Virgin," the weather lady on channel 4, Betty, Veronica, Olive Oyl, the girl in the Sears catalog, Chelsea Clinton, her mom, "The Nanny," Steve's sister, the voice in those airline commercials, the lady in the second window two houses over, the Statue of Liberty chick, and Mrs. Butterworth, I'd be off this rock and on to the next planet.

Mrs. Dubcek -
My Hero

SALLY: IF YOU'RE GOING TO BE THE WOMAN, LEARN FROM THE BEST

I'll never forget the day I drew the assignment of being "the woman" on Earth. I threw my arms around the high commander and whispered, "I am going to squeeze the life out of you for this!" But I didn't. I did what every responsible soldier does: I lay on the floor under my bunk, tears and snot streaming down my face, and cried myself to sleep. When I woke up, their only star was shining warm, golden rays through the window. A tiny creature was making delightful chirping sounds. I threw my shoe at it. It was a new day.

I decided to get on the case and go study the species and gender I had become. Then I got cramps, and I had to go back to bed for a couple of hours. Later that evening I felt a little better, the mood swings were becoming less frequent, and I got down to business. I would study the mannerisms and habits of the female in closest proximity to our apartment—the landlady, Mrs. Dubcek. I wanted to watch her go about her womanly business. The best way to observe her was for me to stay out of sight, so I stealthily cased out the lower level of our living structure and found a small window looking into Mrs. Dubcek's kitchen. She was sitting at the table. In her mouth was one of those paper tubes with dried plants rolled inside. She set fire to the tube and breathed in the smoke, which triggered a hacking cough, an obvious pleasure response. From this spot, I studied my first real woman for three consecutive days.

Day One

DATA

<u>Morning:</u> Pours a citrus fruit drink into a large glass. Takes a sip. Adds clear liquid from a bottle with Russian writing on the label. Drinks quickly. Has three more.

<u>Afternoon:</u> Sleeps.

<u>Evening:</u> Walks around in undergarments. Talks on telephone; accuses someone named Dale of using her credit card again.

Day Two

DATA

<u>Morning:</u> Invites mail carrier in for coffee. Accidentally rips her robe on refrigerator door. Dubcek and mail carrier exit to bedroom. No doubt to repair robe.

<u>Afternoon/Evening:</u> Had assignment in our apartment. Dick brought home something called a "Frisbee." I had to take notes while we observed it.

Day Three

DATA

<u>Morning:</u> Very exciting. Woman with large body and hair molded into a helmet-like form smokes and talks with Dubcek. I am witness to female bonding.

<u>Afternoon:</u> Large woman with hair helmet still in kitchen. Large woman and Dubcek have two hour discussion questioning the integrity of someone called "that Greek bastard."

<u>Evening:</u> Dubcek appears in kitchen layered in sparkly clothing. Has another Russian citrus fruit drink and stumbles out the door to car, apparently driven by aforementioned "Greek bastard."

TRYING IT OUT

If you're lucky enough, as I was, to study the perfect female specimen, imitate her vocal patterns, mannerisms, and clothing choices in a public place. This practice is invaluable in helping you become assimilated in this strange, hostile environment. I chose "Hector's Open-All-Night Grocery," on the corner of Pensdale and Baltic Avenue.

Day Four

DATA

As I entered the store in my ripped floral bathrobe, I noticed the approving smiles from two or three males gathered around the counter. They were obviously convinced I was the real thing. I asked for a bottle of clear Russian liquid and citrus juice, then commenced to accuse the salesclerk of using my charge card without my knowing it. The girl, who could only stare at me with her mouth open, seemed impressed. I turned to the others in the store and in a loud voice asked them if they'd seen "that Greek bastard." I said I'd like to hire someone to kick his ass. For some reason, this caused most people in the store to leave. Having used up all the womanly conversation techniques I had observed from Dubcek, I found myself at a complete loss. I think the salesclerk could tell I was uncomfortable. She was kind enough to remind me that since I had my liquid supplies, I was free to leave the store.

Well, my first time out and, damn it, I was good. Really good. I had been a convincing Earth woman for at least ten minutes. And I'm sure you can be, too.

FIVE RULES ON FITTING IN AMONG THE HUMANS

Humans are a much more complex species than I had anticipated. But after observing them for the past few months, I believe I have come to understand them and their ways. It took us some time to figure this out, but it seems that humans are a social species (who knew?). They settle in large groups known as cities, which deal with each other through a loose system of professional sports teams. Large groups of cities are known as countries, and they deal with each other through a loose system of threats and insults.

It can be intimidating. But pay attention to these five rules on fitting in, and you too will come to be accepted as one of their own. They may even invite you to join one of their secret clubs, many of which sell tapes and CDs at or below retail prices.

RULE #1

Be loud and aggressive whenever possible. Be the center of attention. Dominate conversation. Look people in the eye, kiss them on the lips, and touch them on their . . . well, that one only goes over about 40 percent of the time. But you get the point. It's that kind of planet. The silent loners in society are looked upon with suspicion and often fear. Especially the postal workers (I guess some things are universal).

RULE #2

After a lot of trial and error, I'd say that Rule #2 would have to be: Wear clothes in public. And *keep them on*. Humans are amazingly prudish for a race with such interesting appendages. The concept is not as easy as you might think. Certain areas of the body must be covered at all times, others just during meals and business meetings.

The *only* exceptions to this rule are Demi Moore and her titanium-steel breasts and Michael Douglas and his flabby, doughy ass.

RULE #3

Fresh breath. Not to be confused with morning breath or garlic breath, fresh breath is an absolute must. It can be achieved by several methods. A general rule of thumb: If it smells good, put it in your mouth. Some suggestions are toothpaste, mouthwash, gum, mints, and deodorant spray.

RULE #4

Body language. Posture and bearing say a lot about your attitude and personality (your mouth says the rest). Remember, *The Hunchback of Notre Dame* didn't gross as much as *Aladdin,* who never slouched. Hold your head high (don't use your hands to do it). In fact, keep your hands at your sides and away from any orifices at all times. The excuse, "I was looking for my keys" will not work.

These four rules should let you pass for a human with flying colors, but in the event that you find yourself in over your head, Rule #5 will save the day.

RULE #5

The "Got Your Nose" trick. It's your ace in the hole, a lifesaver that works like magic in any situation. Simple and easy to learn, it's gotten me out of many a close call. Use it anytime you find yourself cornered or at a loss for words.

HUMAN VANITY

One of the great things about Earth is that human technological advancements have made it possible for people to change things about themselves which they don't like. Here are a few of the procedures we have encountered so far.

Breast Augmentation. (Also known as a "boob job," due to the mental level of those who have it done.) The breast is cut open and bags of clear liquid are stuffed in. The breast then loses its soft, pliable consistency and becomes huge and rigid, often taking on the shape of weaponry, hence the phrase "sweater missiles." Clearly the bold, pugnacious appearance of augmented breasts is a sign of strength and pride. They seem to scream, *"Attention! Don't make us knock you off the sidewalk! We'll put your eyes out!"* Other Implants include:

Pectoral Implants. Similar to breast implants, but square.

Chin Implants. A safety measure, to help keep helmets in place.

Collagen Injections. To give the lips a "bee-stung" look, perhaps as a decoy to ward off bee attacks.

Penile Enlargement. This is the only procedure that isn't completely stupid. Not that I need one.

Hair Plugs. Hair is taken from a fertile region and forcibly relocated onto the top of the head. Another option is the synthetic hair, or toupee. In this case, the goal is not to achieve a natural appearance, but rather to call attention to the man-made hair, as if to say, "Look what I can afford!"

Rhinoplasty. Also known as a "nose job." Considering that

Vanity is not an easy talent to acquire. It helps if you're incredibly dashing.

almost all plastic surgery involves making small things larger, this one is a mystery. My theory is that people want to look more like music superstar Michael Jackson, who sadly was born without a nose.

Liposuction. A procedure for women that alleviates a condition known as "cottage cheese thighs." A hose sucks out the cottage cheese, which is then packaged with pineapple, sold in grocery stores, and consumed by women. This would appear to be the very definition of a vicious circle.

Prosthetic Legs. Some people apparently prefer the durability of wood or plastic to traditional meat legs. First popularized by pirates.

OWNING A CAR

Though cars cannot travel interdimensionally—they don't even leave the *surface!*—and are limited to the ludicrously sluggish speed of .000000000013605442 light-years/hour, they are still your best bet for transportation on Earth.

PURCHASING A CAR

There are two kinds of car—new and used. Used are cheaper. The cheapest of all are labeled "As Is" or "Must Go!" That's the kind you want.

When you go to a used-car dealership, you will notice that each car has a price marked prominently on the window. This is not the price of the car.

If you're lucky, like me, the car dealer will take a personal liking to you and give you a special deal. I was doubly lucky, because the day I went to purchase my car happened to coincide with an accidental over-supply of cars on the lot, and I'm not ashamed to admit I used this to my advantage. Because he liked me so much, my dealer Steve led me directly to the best car on the lot (as a car dealer, who would know better than him?), complete with AM radio and polished cow-skin seats.

LEARNING TO DRIVE

If you can drive a spaceship, surely you can drive a *car*. Don't bother with lessons.

DRIVING AS SPORT

One of the fun things about driving is that you can make a nice profit from it. If you are driving and another car hits you from behind, you win his money! So stop short as often as possible.

CAR ALARMS

Of course, you cannot always be with your car. This is why many humans purchase car alarms. Alarms will alert you at any hour of the night when a large truck drives by your car or if a cat jumps on the hood. You can't put a price on that kind of peace of mind.

ALIENS GO HOME

One of the immediate problems with the human body is that you have to put it somewhere. In other words, you will need a place to live. Be careful, there are many hidden pitfalls to renting or buying a home. Here are some examples.

Nice, but ceilings too tall to heat or cool effectively.

Government housing. Carries the stigma of "not doing well."

We considered carefully before moving to our swank digs at 417 Pensdale Drive in beautiful Rutherford, Ohio.

A REALLY BRIEF HISTORY OF TIME

As we well know, time is neither linear nor perceptible. Humans, however, have a curious fear of the intangible, and prefer to live in the past. They often refer to a time known as "The Good Old Days," which seems to be the era immediately before the present one. To familiarize you with their past, here is an appropriately brief history of rather unspectacular "human achievements."

10 billion B.C.

The Medium-sized Bang. Humans overestimate its importance.

200 million B.C.

Dinosaurs rule the world. And didn't do such a bad job of it, considering their pea-sized brains and lack of a well-organized tricameral government.

100 million B.C.

Giant meteor strikes the Earth. Suspiciously around the time Harry came back with that unexplained dent.

1 million B.C.

Homo erectus, a primitive carbon-based life-form, becomes dominant. Australopithecine ape-man taunts him with cries of "Homo!" *Homo erectus* hits him over the head with his purse. Ape-man becomes extinct.

50,000 B.C.

The Ice Age. Great skiing. No crowded lifts.

God creates Man and Woman. Only two sexes, but it's not as limiting as it sounds.

15,000 B.C.

Homo erectus brings fire into the cave. Burns himself. Tells wife to cook with it.

Primitive police respond to first domestic squabble.

10,000 B.C.

Dogs are domesticated by Near Eastern tribespeople. First one is named "Buttons." Ironically, actual buttons not invented for thousands of years.

Man uses first tool. Woman tells him to put it in the garage. Man hangs first Peg-Board.

First man realizes he may already be a millionaire.

7000 B.C.

The wheel is invented. Rolls away.

Wheel invented again. Put on cart. First cart accident two days later.

The Great Flood. Great for fish, maybe. Other species less happy about it.

3000 B.C.

Pyramids are built. The Egyptians don't give us any credit.

1000 B.C.

Wandering man eating peanut butter bumps into sitting man eating choco-late. The foods accidentally mix, and the two men find the combination delightful. Unfortunately, both are killed by tigers and the peanut-butter cup is lost to man for another four millennia.

200 B.C.

Great Wall of China is built. "Great" is rela-tive term.

0

Humans, realizing the "Countdown to the Apocalypse" (hosted by a fellow Dick, Clark) was a bit off, start counting forward as A.D. begins. Thousands of people continue to write "B.C." on their checks for years.

30 A.D.

Jesus dies and is resurrected.

Boredom is discovered.

1000 A.D.

The Holy Wars—or, my God is bigger than yours.

The printing press is invented. First newspaper printed. First headline: "Printing Press Invented."

The Spanish Inquisition. Where are these people's manners?

1500 A.D.

Native Americans discover Spaniards on their beach. Spanish get better media spin on it.

Shakespeare writes his love sonnets. No doubt to an ancestor of Mary Albright.

Theory of gravity finally proposed after an apple falls on someone's head for the first time in history.

1700 A.D.

The Boston Tea Party. Fish don't sleep for weeks.

The Constitution is written. Everyone is created equal. However, size matters.

1800 A.D.

First parachute jump. Further jumps postponed until release cord is invented.

Darwin comes up with theory of natural selection to impress date. Attempt doesn't work, theory does.

The telephone is invented. First obscene call to Bell quickly traced to Watson.

1900 A.D.

Radio is invented. Earth starts bombarding the Universe with laxative commercials.

Motion pictures invented. Jujube stock skyrockets.

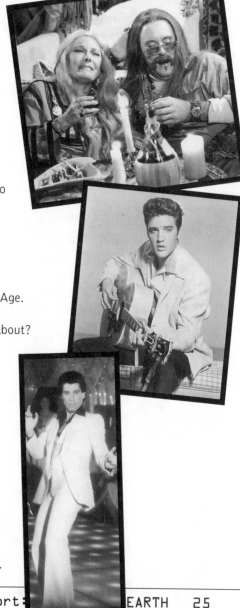

World Wars I and II. Humans finally find something they're good at.

1950 A.D.

Year Mary Albright is born.
Year Mary Albright claims to be born.

Birth control pill is invented. Women search desperately for new excuse not to have sex.

Feminism invented.

1960 A.D.

Television is invented. The second Dark Age.

The sixties. What the hell was that all about?

Man walks on the Moon. Proclaims it a "giant leap for mankind." Picks up a few rocks, hits some golf balls, and goes home. Big deal.

1970 A.D.

Elvis dies and is resurrected.

The Disco Era.

2000 A.D.

Second Great Meteor Crash of . . . whoops. Getting a little ahead of myself.

THE REAL SEVEN WONDERS OF THE WORLD

It has come to my attention that humans, in all their years living on this planet, have decided there are only seven wonders of the world. Ironically, the only "wonder" still in existence are the "Egyptian" pyramids—not much of a surprise considering some of our finest engineers oversaw the project. (Common theory holds that the pyramids were built from the *ground up*. Ha!) In any case, I have found many other "wonders" far superior in ingenuity, practicality, longevity, and beauty to any Hanging Gardens of Babylon . . . which would still be around if they had only watered it.

1   **"THE BOX OF TISSUES"**
     A container full of soft, two-ply, often quilted, sometimes lotioned sheets of paper used to blow the nose (or for emergency purposes when toilet paper runs out). One sheet protrudes from a slit at the top of the box, and when pulled out, another soft, two-ply, often quilted, sometimes lotioned sheet appears *in the same location*. When this sheet is used, another follows. And another, ad infinitum. This entire cycle could take days, months, years, or minutes (depending on the liquidity of your nose—or how fast you run out of toilet paper).

2   **"THE WONDER BREAD"**
     Soft, two-ply, often quilted, sometimes lotioned pieces of white bread. Great if you run out of tissues.

3   **"THE PENCIL SHARPENER"**
     A "pencil" is a writing instrument consisting of lead encompassed by a sheath of wood. When the lead dulls after usage, it can be placed into an electric hole. When the pencil is pulled out of the

electric hole, it has been "unblunted." Does not work with pens. Does not work with carrots. (Should be renamed "Pencil Unblunterer.")

4   "THE TRASH"

When things get old and/or begin to emit an acrid odor, they take on a new name: "Trash." It is an all-inclusive word: Bananas can become trash. Phones can become trash. White people can become trash. When something becomes trash, it must be "thrown away" (or placed in a location other than where it is). For example, if there is a rotten tuna sandwich on my desk, it is suggested I put it someplace else other than my desk (i.e., on Dr. Albright's desk). Everything on this planet turns to trash. How wonderful.

SUBJECT

Places to Avoid While on Earth

DATA

1. Yahoo Serious Film Festivals.
2. The Happy Brand sausage factory tour.
3. All-white jazz ensembles.
4. Public men's rooms in subway stations.
5. All-you-can-eat buffets at strip joints.

5   "THE THERMOS BOTTLE"

No, it doesn't much surprise me that a Thermos bottle keeps hot things hot and cold things cold. But what amazes me is that the cap on top turns into a cup. *A cup!* Brilliant!

6   "THE CORDUROY"

A dense fabric which is both soft yet durable, hardy yet flexible. A dichotomy of knitted fibers woven together in an alternating pattern of high and low points. When worn, corduroy (or "cords," as the hipsters refer to it) seems to reflect the internal emotions of the wearer, whether it be lazy or vibrant, coy or stoic. Corduroy is most certainly the mood ring of fabrics. (Note: Harry likes to rub his face against it.)

7   "THE 'EGYPTIAN' PYRAMIDS"

Of course.

2 Relationships

eautiful

ng, then

unding
e.

d. When
answer,

HOW TO PLEASURE A HUMAN

There are a few activities you *must* experience while on Earth. Right up at the top of the must-do list are:

1. Eat a quart of ice cream. I'm serious. It's an amazing experience. You'll especially enjoy the "brain freeze," wherein your entire head goes numb.

2. Eat a quart of Ben & Jerry's New York Super Fudge Chunk ice cream. Even better.

3. Have sex with a human.

Having sex with a human is the most fun, but also the most difficult to achieve. Ice cream you can just go downtown and purchase. Actually, you can just go downtown and purchase sex, too, but the women are poorly dressed, as well as disconcertingly forward.

Besides, with sex, the pursuit is half the fun. Well, not half. Perhaps a third. A tenth. Okay, it's hell, and it will keep you awake nights, gnawing at your very soul. But man oh man is it worth it when you "score."

The first step toward having sex is to . . .

FALL IN LOVE

This will happen immediately after you arrive, if you pick good landing coordinates. Bad coordinates include maximum security men's prisons (no women), maternity hospitals (the women have all already had sex), and lakes (you will drown).

Pendleton State University was a perfect choice. Why? It is home to Dr. Mary Albright, and within hours I was drawn to her like a moth to a magnet.

It takes a lot of finesse to let a human woman know of your intentions without scaring her off. First impressions are crucial, so you should be armed with what we on Earth call . . .

Dr. Albright squirts me with water: A curious yet refreshing aspect of the mating ritual.

OPENING LINES

Your first approach must be romantic without being too aggressive, direct and yet coy. For instance:

"You make me feel like I've never seen a human woman before." (She doesn't have to know it's true!)

"I don't know which zodiac sign is known to be the most beautiful and wonderful, but I bet you're it."

"Can I buy you a drink, then dinner, then an engagement ring, then a house, then children, then a coffin?"

"If I can't have you, I'll set myself on fire in your front yard."

Then you're on your way. Just a few months of constant hounding and desperate pleading, and you'll be going out on your first date.

THE "DATE"

Yes, that's what it's called. But don't make the mistake I did. When a woman says, "Are you trying to ask me out on a date?" Don't answer, "Yes. October twenty-seventh." What she means is not a calendar date, but a social excursion. Think of a date as a sort of mating ritual where money is exchanged instead of fluids.

Where to on the date? A very tricky question indeed. Women are very hard to read, and the slightest distinction can make the difference between a night you'll remember and a night she won't let you forget. Let my experience with Dr. Albright illustrate how fine the line is.

Yes, there will be dates that don't go perfectly. There will be awkward moments. There will be months where she won't speak to you or make eye contact. But when the magic finally happens, it's all worthwhile.

SUBJECT	
Good Date Ideas	Bad Date Ideas

DATA	
Romantic film	Pornographic film
Wedding	Wedding of total strangers
Cat show	Cat fight
Art exhibit	Body-art exhibit
Auto show	Autopsy
Drive in the country	Drive in the lake
Rent a videotape	Rent a Ditch Witch
Modern dance	Lap dance
Champagne brunch	Beer breakfast

An admiring glance is always an effective way to melt a woman's heart.

An excellent precursor to sex is watching other people have sex. This is called foreplay.

THE ACT OF SEX

It's not like back home. You don't just launch a capsule of proto-plasm into your partner's receptor port and wait for the impact summary. No, Earth sex involves direct, prolonged physical contact: cuddling, grappling, heaving, collapsing, and, for her, spasms of giggling.

Describing the act itself to the uninitiated would be difficult. Therefore, I am sending you all a videotape of myself and Dr. Albright having sex. (She doesn't know anything about it yet. I'm going to surprise her by premiering it at her birthday party!) Watch and enjoy!

If a picture could speak a thousand words...

TOMMY'S GUIDE TO STARING AT THE BODY OF A TYPICAL HIGH SCHOOL CHEERLEADER

A high school girl's body is divided into four quadrants:

1. Staring anywhere at the body parts in the FIRST QUADRANT is perfectly acceptable. You can even compliment first quadrant body parts (i.e., "Gee, your hair smells terrific."). Though poking or pulling any first quadrant body parts is frowned upon.

2. The SECOND QUADRANT is *completely* off-limits, although it's definitely the most tempting. Almost everything really cool is located in the second quadrant. So if you want to look, make absolutely sure she can't tell. But if she catches you, make up some excuse (i.e., "I wasn't staring at your breasts. I didn't notice you even had any!").

3. THIRD QUADRANT body parts are boring from the front, but there's a great surprise in the back. Look all you want, she'll never know. As long as she doesn't turn around and catch you. Or she's wearing glasses with a stupid rear-view mirror. Pinching is not acceptable. But fun fun fun!

4. Body parts in the FOURTH QUADRANT are long, smooth, and exciting. Stare until your eyes dry out, she'll just think you're looking at the floor. When toenails are polished bright red, it makes things twice as exciting. When high heels are being worn, watch out—chances are she wants you.

SALLY'S GUIDE TO DATING

A large part of the human experience seems to focus on the opposite sex. Everything humans do revolves around this. Women dress nicely to attract men, stay in shape to attract men, work to have money in order to attract men, behave "badly" to attract men, and pretend like they don't care about men to attract men. (In fact, almost anything a woman does attracts men.)

Women devote enormous amounts of energy on figuring out how exactly to "land a rich guy." After much trial and error (mostly error), I've come up with a simple system that guarantees complete success or your money back.

1   The first aspect of getting men is knowing where to find them. This is simply a matter of finding out where they gather. I suggest sporting events, car auctions, locker rooms, strip clubs, prisons, and anyplace where prostates are examined.

2   Once you've discovered where to meet men, you now need to approach them. A word of caution here: Stay away from men who are already taken. They're not hard to spot—they're usually twenty pounds overweight and look like they've lost their will to live. Once you've determined that the man is available, you are now ready to proceed. The key here is a good pickup line. Here are a few that have worked wonders for me:

A.   Your cologne smells so good it makes me want to cry.

B.   Hi, you have a lot of hair.

C.   Excuse me, are those nuts salted? (Make sure a bowl of nuts is present when you use this one.)

D.   Hi, I'm looking for someone to have sex with.

E.   I think your genitalia are in diametric opposition to mine.

3 Once you've made initial contact, it's time for the first date. You want to impress him here, so make sure you take a shower first. And dress appropriately. The typical date uniform should consist of a dress that hugs the body, collecting the chest and thrusting it forward. A rule on skirt length: Stand with your arms at your sides. If your hands fall naturally at your hemline, it is *too long*. Now that you're dressed, you're ready to go out. It is probably a good idea not to eat before the date, since he will probably want to take you to dinner. (You know what they say, the way to a woman's heart is through her stomach.) Just a warning, "all you can eat" means all you can eat *at that time*.

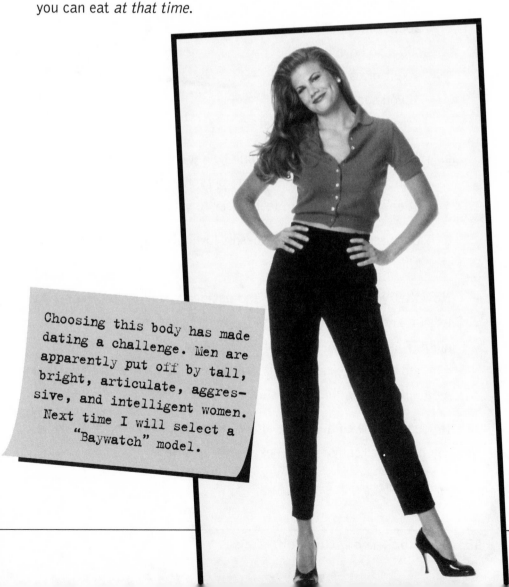

Choosing this body has made dating a challenge. Men are apparently put off by tall, bright, articulate, aggressive, and intelligent women. Next time I will select a "Baywatch" model.

4   When you are on a first date, things can get a bit awkward, so you want to keep talking at all times. Here are some icebreakers to keep the conversation lively and exciting:

A.   If you've had sex, tell him about it. And don't leave out any of the details. It shows you're a real woman.

B.   Ask him if he's had sex. And if so, with how many people. This is good because it gets him talking about himself, and if you also have had sex, it gives the two of you something in common right from the start.

NOTE:
Beware of blind dates. They are rarely actually blind, and usually have much bigger problems. (See section on faking sudden illnesses.)

C.   Tell him that your uterine lining sloughs itself every twenty-eight days. Sharing something personal like this will put him at ease and make him feel closer to you.

D.   Discuss weaponry. Who doesn't love a hearty debate on how to kill?

5   Now that you've had the date and decided you like him, you need to let him know. Try sitting across from his house in your car late at night. This will be your way of telling him that you're thinking of him and are concerned for his safety. Also, call him five or six times a day just to say "hi." He's sure to be flattered.

If you've followed all of the above suggestions and you still like him, you might be ready for the next step—marriage.

MARRIAGE

The end result of all that dating. The idea is that two people fall in love and commit to one another for "all eternity" (that's considered a long time on this planet). Getting married is considered to be one of the most important things to accomplish.

In order to get married, there first must be an engagement period, where the couple sees if they are compatible by trying to agree on china patterns and kitchen utensils. Then there is the ceremony. It's called a wedding, and it starts with the bride (the girl) being given away, like an object, to the groom (the man). (Note: The female does not devour the male after the ceremony. That happens during what they call the "divorce.")

When you get married, you are, in effect, entering a legally binding contract. In it, there are strict rules of conduct that you agree to follow:

1   You are not allowed to have sex with anyone but each other.

2   You stop having sex with each other after the first year.

3   You wear a wedding ring so other people know you are married. (Note: A wedding ring appears to make you more attractive to people looking for wild, uninhibited, no-strings-attached sex. Unfortunately, Rule #1 prohibits capitalizing on this. Come to think of it, Rule #2 makes this suck big-time.)

4   You agree to be totally honest with each other, except when she asks about her weight, in which case you both agree you are to lie.

5   You have the right to break wind in front of each other without apology.

FRIENDS—HOW TO MAKE THEM LIKE YOU

As Earth lacks the Sycophant Droid Squad of home, it can become a very lonely place if you don't make friends with other earthlings. (Note: Humans often refer to dogs as "man's best friend," so blissfully unaware are they of what dogs *really* think of them.) Best of all, friends can drive you to the airport and help you move.

HOW TO MAKE FRIENDS WITH SOMEONE

Once you've found someone you want to be befriend, try the following approaches to gaining his friendship:

- Give him money.

- Offer him a nice steak.

- Rescue him from an enemy POW camp. (This is most effective during wartime.)

NICKNAMES

All humans have names assigned to them at birth. This is much less efficient than our own numbering system, which prevents duplication and also such names as "Brandon" and "Wesley." As if this designation system were not sufficiently confusing on its own, most humans also have what are known as "nicknames." You'll find you become closer with your friend if you call him by a nickname. Suggested nicknames include:

"Stretch"—if your friend is tall.

"Tubby"—if your friend is overweight.

"Fatso"—if your friend is very overweight.

"Huge Fat Tub of Lard"—if your friend is really extremely overweight.

"Charlie"—if your friend's name is Charles.

"Wombat"—if your friend is a wombat.

"Satchmo"—if your friend is the late Louis Armstrong.

"Booger"—trust me, you don't want to know.

3 Food and Maintenance

Dinky
ag him
all if he

THE HIGH COMMANDER'S RESTAURANT GUIDE

You may have noticed that our Earth home, as all Earth homes, is equipped with a food preparation area called a kitchen. However, its purpose seems to be primarily decorative. We've never met anyone who uses their kitchen, and Sally has determined that the oven actually burns everything you put in it. No, humans do 99 percent of their eating in restaurants.

Rutherford may not be the largest city on Earth—in fact, I've seen a city on TV called "California" that appears to be much larger—but it does have a remarkable diversity of restaurant dining options.

THE HIGH COMMANDER'S "QUALIRATE" QUALITY RATING SYSTEM©

✖✖✖✖	= 4	✖✖	= 2
✖✖✖	= 3	✖	= 1

SUBJECT

McDonald's

DATA

Location: 1802 Flagler Parkway

Hours: 7 a.m. to midnight, seven days a week

✖✖✖✖

The grande dame of Rutherford dining. Hamburgers are the centerpiece of the menu, but hamburgers are just the beginning. From fried potatoes to fried pies, from fried fish to fried nuggets of chicken, there is no flavor of international cuisine that doesn't have a home in their gleaming vats of oil.

Has this formula added up to success? You bet it has. There are just sixteen tables, plus a drive-through, and yet they have served literally 99 billion meals! How popular is that in Earth terms? It means every man, woman, and child in Rutherford has eaten 1.65 million hamburgers in their lifetime. Mr. McDonald has such a winning formula here, it's a shame he hasn't opened additional branches. Of course, the fact that he is a circus clown with appalling orange hair may make it difficult for him to find backers.

SUBJECT

The Hospital Cafeteria

DATA

Location: Rutherford Memorial Hospital
2000 Hospital Drive

Hours: 24 hours a day, seven days a week!

✗ ✗ ✗

From our experience, "hospital food" is synonymous with "good eatin'!" The smell greets your nose the moment you enter the emergency room, and not even the acrid stench of ammonia, blood, and decaying flesh can mask it.

The thing that distinguishes the cuisine at the hospital cafeteria is the presentation. Every dish is laid out in identical stainless steel bins, with identical steel spoons, at an identical temperature: piping hot! And this delectable sense of order continues in the texture of the food itself. Macaroni, potatoes au gratin, peach cobbler, meatloaf—each is distinguished by a smooth, comforting mealiness and topped off with a dry, crispy crust.

A Note of Warning: For some reason, the cafeteria's food attracts those disgusting jiggly creatures we encountered on the brown planet—here, they call them "Jell-O's"—and they're always loitering around the dessert table. We have repeatedly asked the management to ban them from the cafeteria, but have only met with bemused indifference. Jell-O's must tip well.

SUBJECT

Pinky Dinky Ice Cream Truck

DATA

Location: Constantly changing

✗ ✗

Perhaps the oddest eating experience in Rutherford, the Pinky Dinky man just drives around, forcing you to literally chase him and flag him down to buy his delicious frozen treats. You'd never find him at all if he didn't play his radio so loudly.

WHAT TO DO WHEN YOU ENCOUNTER JELL-O.

Sometimes, when you least expect it, you will encounter Jell-O. Don't panic. You can escape unharmed if you follow a few guidelines.

1   Never let it see you're afraid. Jell-O loves this.

2   Smile. Say you are a friend, you come in peace.

3   Reason with it.

4   Offer it a gift.

5   Find out what it wants.

6   Let it see you have no weapons.

7   If it continues to jiggle menacingly, stab it to death with a kitchen knife and throw it in the sink.

HOW TO SELECT YOUR MORNING BREAKFAST CEREAL BY HARRY SOLOMON

Choosing a breakfast cereal can be a very befuddling experience. For instance, Alphabits have K's in them, but Special K hasn't got any K's. I swear! The first thing you have to do is figure out where they keep the boxes. This involves steering your way through a terrifying gauntlet of aisles. You'll know you've reached the cereal aisle because it's guarded by strange beasts, tigers, and, scariest of all, Quakers. Here is a guide to help you make the most important decision of your entire life.

COCOA PUFFS

At first I scoffed at the notion of going "cuckoo" for Cocoa Puffs. The mental patient on the box made me think twice. After all, a person must safeguard his sanity at all costs. His was a cautionary tale. But I took home a box anyway. After eating, I'll admit I felt a little light-headed. Nonetheless, now that I am once again in sound mind and body, I must commend General Mills and his entire infantry for such a delightful chocolate treat.

LUCKY CHARMS

Being a devout fan of the movies *Leprechaun I* and *Leprechaun II*, I was intrigued with the notion of using a murderous Irish dwarf to sell cereal to children. While I'll admit the green clovers had a certain je ne sais quoi, I found the yellow moons quite pedestrian and the pink hearts positively amateurish.

FROOT LOOPS

I took special pleasure in the delightful tropical motif on the box, but I did find the maze on the back insultingly easy. And the name of the toucan, "Sam," really put me off.

TRIX

Will someone please give the rabbit some Trix. It's just too cruel. Also, why do they have him on the box if he's never tasted the stuff?

LIFE

Avoid this cereal. I ate a whole box, and I still don't have one.

Banana Muffins

Makes between one and two hundred, depending on how big you make 'em.

What You Need:

~~54 dozen eggs~~

A lot of sugar (the more the better)

5 lbs. flour (or you can substitute more sugar)

2 bananas

eat oven to 350 degrees. Or whatever. Put a
trainer in a bowl. Throw eggs into strainer.
ash well.

Dump in all the other stuff, especially the bananas, and mix until your arm hurts. Take out the muffin cup holder from the pantry. Remove dead cockroaches from muffin cup holder. Pour gunk from bowl into muffin craters and shove into the oven.

Wait until they're done, then remove. Mmmm ... good muffins. Sprinkle a little sugar on top for some extra-sugary muffins.

Garnish with parsley.

Cheesecake

This is probably the best recipe I've got. I know this for a fact, because I hate cheesecake.

What You Need:

Any kind of premade cake (any kind)

2 lbs. cheese (any kind, in chunks)

5 sticks butter

Heat oven to 350 degrees. Take premade cake and cover with butter. Place the chunks of cheese into the butter so that the cheese covers the entire cake evenly. Lick fingers (thumb first!), then stick cake in oven until the cheese bubbles and the whole thing bakes to a crisp.

Remove cake from oven. Poke with toothpick. If toothpick breaks instantly, then cake's ready. Sprinkle with sugar. (Suggestion: Serve with orange soda.)

Garnish with parsley.

Five Layer Cake

Fun, easy to make, and tall!

What You Need:

A car

Key to aforementioned car

Heat oven to 350 degrees. Get in car. Turn key. Drive straight to nearest store and buy *six* cakes and a box of clear toothpicks. When you get home, stick clear toothpicks into five of the cakes and jam each cake into each other (the clear toothpicks will act as nails). It takes a while to get this thing just right, so eat the sixth cake while you're working.

Turn off oven. Drizzle sugar liberally over the whole cake. Slice and serve with chopped parsley.

Eight-Course French Dinner

This is easier than it looks!

What You Need:

A telephone

A French-English dictionary

A watch with a minute hand

Some money

Call a take-out pizza place and order a pie. When it arrives, check your watch. If it has taken longer than thirty minutes to arrive, then it's free. If not, take the money and pay the delivery person. Cut the pizza into eight slices. Demand everyone speak French.

Serve with parsley.

While the "men" sit around the kitchen table, it is my job as a woman to feed them. The dish towel over the shoulder is an indispensable accessory.

HARRY'S ADVICE NOBODY TELLS YOU

Be forewarned: Taking on the form of a human body can be hazardous to your health. Although beautiful, the human body is also irrevocably flawed. For one, its head can be chopped off. And it can stub its toe. But worst of all, it will invariably catch a cold.

If you are planning to have surgery to repair any damage, here are some do's and don'ts to make you experience a successful one.

1. Do not "hide" your pills and ask the nursing staff to find them.

2. Do not call the Big Giant Head a "fruitcake" while under anesthesia.

3. Do not request elective head surgery.

4. Do not insist that there is such a thing as recreational enemas and you want one "right now!"

While a stay at the local "hospital" brings promise of excellent cuisine, it's a good idea to stay healthy and away from it—the "blood pressure" cuffs are murder.

SALLY'S GUIDE TO EARTH HAIR—HOW TO GROW IT AND WHEN TO SHAVE IT

As men and women on Earth evolved, they went through a kind of molting process. The majority of hair that once covered their entire bodies fell out and was replaced with the fur from less fortunate creatures. The only remaining hair on modern men and women covers what are considered the most vulnerable parts of the human body. One of the poorest design concepts of the human body has to be this: hair as protection.

WHERE TO LOOK FOR HAIR

THE SCALP

This is where I'd say vulnerable body-part coverage is the thickest. Humans love the hair on their heads. More than protection, it has become, along with fingernails, an amazing organic decoration. The individuals most obsessed with their hair seem to be the female species and former NFL players turned sports announcers. Preventing hair from leaving their heads is the obsession of males. Maybe they don't want to show up the gals by evolving further.

There are businesses set up all over the world that cater to the cutting, combing, molding, curling, straightening, and coloring of scalp hair. It's mandatory that the names of these establishments conceal the function of the shop, such as "Curl Up And Dye," "Blood Sweat And Shears," and, most ominously of all, "Mr. Jerry's."

I have surmised that periodically the employees of these hair-chopping places hold a secret meeting. There a "Supreme Haircutter" or "King of the Stylists" dictates a specific haircut that will be forced on all who enter the shops.

THE ARMPITS AND LEGS

Although hair is usually abundant on the armpits and legs of most women, it is considered unsightly and society demands they remove it. It must be shaven with a razor specifically made for women. These razors are packaged in multiples and are named after a flower. When the blade begins to rust, be aware that you can only use it for another month.

Men are allowed to keep underarm hair, leg hair, and just about any other hair that grows on their bodies. Perhaps this is societal compensation for their impending loss of scalp hair. I think women shave off some of their hair just to make men feel better. "See, honey? I don't have much hair either." This is just something I came up with. I could be wrong.

THE PUBIC AREA

Although considered the most valuable and fun area of both the male and female human body, the pubic hair serves no protective purpose at all. Believe me, I made a quick stop on Harry's bike and it hurt like hell. Here the hair is purely decorative (until it turns gray). Then no one wants to look at it. Not even the grower.

Once again, women are urged to control this growth. Not by completely shaving it (unless it's a special occasion or holiday), but by containing it within the margins of their bikini briefs. Jutting hair is considered vulgar and very unfeminine. Women abhor these tenacious follicles so much that they pay to have them ripped out with hot wax again and again. I suspect they're angry at the lack of protection the pubic hair provides.

Men can either shave them off, keep them, or not grow them at all. I think it's pretty obvious that men can do any damn thing they please with whatever hair they have left. (I've only seen one mustached woman. She sold tomatoes out of the back of a truck.)

SPECIAL NOTE: In the elderly human, particularly men, "surprise hen hair," coarse and unruly, will sprout from the ears and nose. I've never seen hair sprouting from the mouth, which leads me to believe once this happens the elderly are shut away out of sight. This Earth can be a cruel place.

y

ar-
od

to

max
hem.

ls.

ill have

aths

your

ngerous

NT

Sometimes we must entertain ourselves. I've been told I play quite a mean mandolin.

MOVIES: SIT BACK, RELAX, ENJOY THE SHOW

When on Earth, be sure to go to the movies. They're a great place to go with your friends to socialize. (Note: You should not speak to or in any way acknowledge your companions while at the movies.) Movies take you to faraway lands. (Note: You do not actually go to any faraway lands while at the movies.) They take you on great adventures. (Note: All adventures are simulated. Some are not so great.)

The content of films varies widely, with a few genres dominating the cinema. The basic elements to look for when choosing a film are *sex* and *violence.*

Violence is found in every movie. It comes in all the colors of the rainbow and provides an excellent overview of the many creative ways to extinguish humans:

Explosions: The murder method of choice for madmen. When an explosion occurs, all people and cars in the area go flying into the air. The bad guys will die a grisly death while the hero will survive unscathed save for some minor soot or grease markings.

Gunfire: Small projectiles of metal are propelled into a person via a handheld mechanism. Once a person's body contains twenty or more, they die. Bad guys, even trained assassins, are surprisingly poor shots and nearly always miss the hero, who, even shooting blindly, will find his target.

Car Crashes: Cars chase each other until one car goes out of control. A metal pole plunges through the windshield and into a person's head.

Knives: Generally, they go into a person's back, and you don't know it until their eyes go wide and they spit up a little blood. Occasionally, though, a knife flies across the room and sticks in a person's throat.

Kung Fu: Ancient Chinese art of kicking a person to death. Usually performed while wearing pajamas.

Arnold: A killing machine. "Arnold" is not an actor, but rather an unbelievably expensive special effect with a curiously dysfunctional voice box. Even the people who claim he is human will tell you he is not an actor.

Sex in movies bears no resemblance to actual human copulation whatsoever, which is why you don't just stay home. Prominent types of movie sex include:

Romantic Sex: The people are really in love, which is suggested by blowing curtains, soft light, gauzy clothing, and nearly continuous female orgasms.

Crazy Sex: An uncontrollable state of lust characterized by the participants tearing perfectly good clothes and throwing perfectly good dishes off the table so they can immediately have sex on it. Acted out with great enthusiasm by Mickey Rourke.

Hooker Sex: Hooker sex is inevitably interrupted by people with guns who riddle the man with bullets (see "Gunfire" above). This causes the hooker to shriek. Oddly, no movie of this type has yet to feature Hugh Grant or Charlie Sheen.

Teen Sex: Similar to "Romantic Sex," but fails to reach climax thanks to the intervention of a mysterious figure who kills them.

RATINGS

G   Reserved exclusively for cartoons and talking animals.

PG   Designed to trick children into coming, thinking it will have nudity or profanity. It won't.

PG-13   Designed to allow thirteen-year-olds to see grisly deaths without being exposed to damaging sex scenes.

R   Guaranteed to have plenty of sex and/or violence, or your money back.

NC-17   Designed to keep young people from seeing truly dangerous material, such as lesbianism or black comedians.

WARNING SIGNS

You can avoid unpleasant moviegoing experiences by keeping clear of the following types of films:

- Any movie with Demi Moore naked.

- Any movie a critic calls "delicious."

- Movies where "anything can happen . . . and usually does!"

- Any movie beginning with the word "die" and ending with the words "hard with a vengeance."

- Any movie with Demi Moore clothed.

- Any movie beginning with the word "Batman."

- Any movie with a dwarf speaking with a British accent.

CRITICS

Film criticism brings up all sorts of interesting questions. When Siskel and Ebert put "two thumbs way up," where do they go? Do two thumbs beat three stars? Can a film critic be drummed out of the business for giving a film an eleven on a scale of one to ten? And if not, why not?

THE MOVIE EXPERIENCE

Before the main feature begins, there will be several short films (also known as "trailers") shown. Typically, much longer versions of these films (known as "features") arrive in theaters several weeks later, but they're never as good.

MOVIES—AN IMPORTANT LEARNING TOOL

Many valuable lessons can be learned from watching movies.

- You can dodge machine-gun fire by running sideways.

- You can avoid injury in exploding cities by hiding in a closet.

- While an F-5 tornado can uproot a house or a tractor, it will not affect you as long as you are holding on to something.

- You should become evil. Evil people are able to spring back to life after being killed, usually two or three times.

- If you break up with your girlfriend, don't worry: Estranged couples can be reunited by the outbreak of a plague, the annihilation of a couple billion earthlings by flying saucers, or really heavy winds.

- If someone walks up to you and says something witty—like "Time to take out the trash" or "You were expecting the Easter Bunny?"—they are about to kill you.

SEQUELS

Some stories are too sweeping and epic to be contained in a single film. Hence the seven *Police Academy* films. Recommended sequels include *Apollo 13*, *X*, and *The Seventh Seal*. More than a decade after the movie *10* was released, the movie *Seven* came out. This is what's called a "prequel."

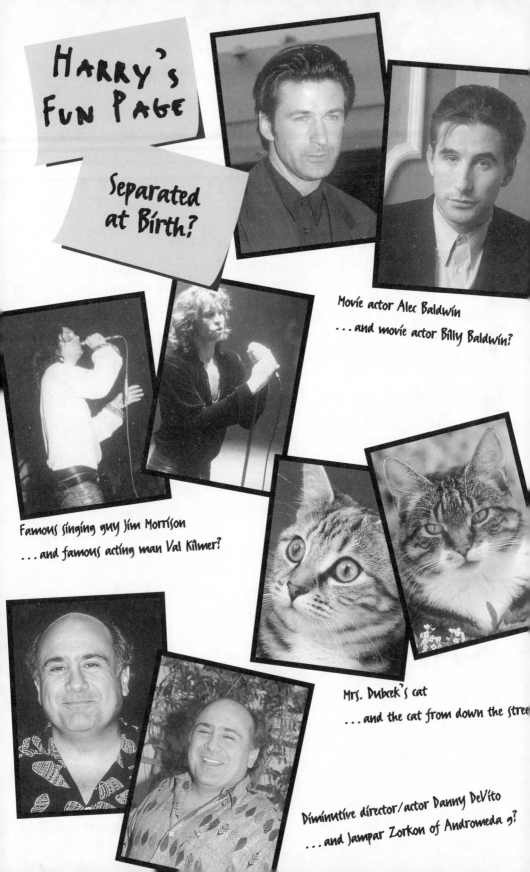

Harry's Fun Page

Separated at Birth?

Movie actor Alec Baldwin
...and movie actor Billy Baldwin?

Famous singing guy Jim Morrison
...and famous acting man Val Kilmer?

Mrs. Dubcek's cat
...and the cat from down the stree

Diminutive director/actor Danny DeVito
...and Jampar Zorkon of Andromeda 9?

THE VIDEO STORE

A few months after movies have played in the theaters, they are transferred to videotape. Then you can go to the video store, rent them, and keep them at your house for seven or eight days. I like to keep a list on my refrigerator of films I want to watch. This way, when I return from the video store I can remember what tapes I forgot to rent.

The store is arranged in alphabetical order. Except for "X" which has its own room. The X-rated films are not as lavishly produced as the others, but what is surprising is that many of the popular films are based on them. For example, *Jewel of the Nile* was inspired by the XXX romp *Tool of the Nile* and *On Golden Blonde* inspired the multiple Academy Award winner *On Golden Pond*.

DICK'S CAPSULE VIDEO REVIEWS

SUBJECT

Friday the 13th

DATA

QualiRate Quality Rating: 2
An insipid, predictable exercise in horror. Notable only for its special effects.

SUBJECT

Friday the 13th Part 2

DATA

QualiRate Quality Rating: 9
An intoxicating trip into the eeriest corners of the dark side of the macabre. Truly a thinking man's horror film.

SUBJECT

Friday the 13th Part 3

DATA

QualiRate Quality Rating: 3
A four-hankie sugar-coated weepathon. If you resent having your emotions manipulated by a director for ninety-six minutes, you'll resent this movie.

SUBJECT

Friday the 13th: The Final Chapter

DATA

QualiRate Quality Rating: 10
A touching family drama, with fully formed characters you really want to root for. Stand up and cheer through your tears! Then sit down, but be prepared to keep cheering.

SUBJECT

Friday the 13th Part V

DATA

QualiRate Quality Rating: 8
One of the few films you'll see this year that can truly be described as erotic. It will literally steam up your living room.

SUBJECT

Friday the 13th Part VI

DATA

QualiRate Quality Rating: Bomb
An utter waste of film. If this is what passed for comedy in the 1980s, remind me not to go there.

SUBJECT

Friday the 13th Part VII

DATA

QualiRate Quality Rating: 11
The sweeping majesty of this film has to be seen on the big screen to be fully appreciated. Restores your faith in the power of film to change the world. Your eyes will literally pop out of your head.

While I must admit I make quite an attractive "woman," I've discovered breasts are more fun to look at than wear.

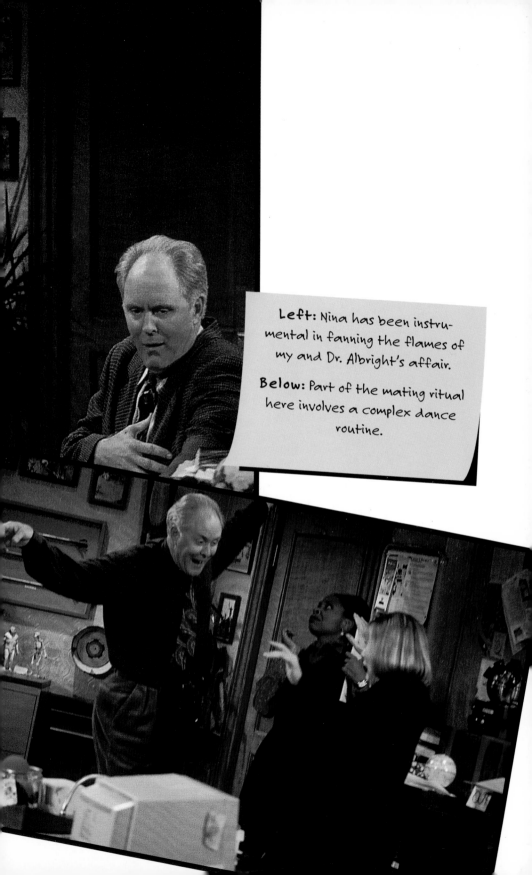

Left: Nina has been instrumental in fanning the flames of my and Dr. Albright's affair.

Below: Part of the mating ritual here involves a complex dance routine.

...it's a real turn-off in
the bedroom.

Photos are fun to look at and even more fun to eat!

Harry with our wise landlady, Mrs. Dubcek. A woman who dispenses some wisdom and collects rent.

I believe this is Harry
sleepwalking. But then again,
how can you tell?

Sally has struggled with her female form, but according to most males, she seems to be winning.

Above: As Sally has experienced, the seemingly innocuous task of making meat loaf can leave dead cow on your hands.

Right: Sally complaining that being a woman is hard "work." As if cooking and cleaning were more physically taxing than the vigors of racquetball!

In one of my many studies and experiments, I discover tissue paper is one of the true seven wonders of this planet.

Tommy Solomon: oozing teenager or elderly information officer?

Harry receiving a transmission
from the Big Giant Head.
We're so proud.

Smoking—it tastes good and it's good for you! There are some minor drawbacks—blackened teeth, bleeding gums, and you might lose a lung or two.

Harry displays his ID card, critical to gaining access to government buildings (such as libraries), operating their primitive motor vehicles, and buying liquor for minors.

Friday the 13th Part VIII

DATA

QualiRate Quality Rating: 2
A cynical attempt to cash in on the success of VII. Literally a cookie-cutter movie, which feels as if it were figuratively made up of pieces of film found in the editing room.

SUBJECT

Jason Goes to Hell: The Final Friday

DATA

QualiRate Quality Rating: 9
Less a film than a deconstructionist essay on the nature of horror. Slow-moving, but thought-provoking, and literally directed by Adam Marcus.

A PARENT'S GUIDE TO RESPONSIBLE VIEWING

It's a wide, wonderful world of movies out there, but I've learned that not all movies are suitable for all people. Therefore I, Harry Solomon, have taken it upon myself to help you become a responsible earthling parent by navigating the treacherous terrain known as "the Multiplex" . . .

FREE WILLY

Recommendation: Children 18 and up only

A giant shark tries to eat a small boy for ninety sadistic minutes.

SHOWGIRLS

Recommendation: Ages 5 and up

The dance sequences will dazzle young and old alike.

MR. HOLLAND'S OPUS

Recommendation: Ages 12 and up

Smaller children will be upset by this tragic tale of a man who ages by thirty years in just two hours and ten minutes.

INDEPENDENCE DAY

Recommendation: Not for anyone of any age

Portrays aliens as cold-blooded murderers who slaughter humans by the thousands. An outrageous stereotype. If this movie wins an Oscar, I'm going to blow up Cleveland! Um, after I ask everyone to evacuate in a safe, orderly fashion.

TAKEN FROM BEHIND 4

Recommendation: Ages 8 and up

The inspirational story of an athletic gardener who becomes romantically involved with five high-society ladies. Only caveat: The prolonged, graphic sex scenes may bore younger children.

SUBJECT
ROCKY IV AND STAR TREK IV: A COMPARISON

DATA

ROCKY IV	STAR TREK IV: THE VOYAGE HOME
PLOT: Rocky goes to the U.S.S.R. to fight a huge Russian boxer.	PLOT: Nobody named Rocky goes to the U.S.S.R. to fight a huge Russian boxer.
SONG: "Eye of the Tiger"	SONG: Suspicious lack of "Eye of the Tiger."
FEMALE STAR: Talia Shire	FEMALE STAR: For a minute, I thought I saw Talia Shire, but now I'm pretty sure it wasn't her.
MORAL: If you believe in yourself, you can go to the U.S.S.R. and fight a huge Russian boxer.	MORAL: Same (except for the part about being able to fight a huge Russian boxer).

Did You Know?????

1. That *Rocky V* is not five times greater than *Rocky I*?

2. That *Rocky I* + *Rocky V* = *Rocky II* x *Rocky III*?

3. That *Rocky V* - *Rocky I* = *Rocky III* + *Rocky I*?

4. That *Rocky IV* x *Rocky V* = (*Rocky III*)³ - *Rocky II* - *Rocky V*?

5. That *Lawnmower Man II* x *Friday the 13th VI* = *Rocky III* x *Halloween III* + *Die Hard III*?

HARRY THE COUCH CRITIC,
OR
TELEVISION SHOWS ANALYZED

SHOW	COMPLAINT	SUGGESTED FIX
"The Odd Couple"	One is neat, the other is sloppy.	Kill the neat one.
"Friends"	None of the friends are ghosts.	Make the Chandler character a wisecracking ghost.
"Silver Spoons"	Too funny!!!	Edit many of the more hilarious jokes.
"Mork and Mindy"	Real aliens don't steal jokes from stand-ups.	Compensate victims' families.
"M*A*S*H*"	Is it just me, or would it have been funnier set at a racetrack?	Compromise by having them operate on racehorses.
"NYPD Blue"	Why must I see Sipowicz's naked behind?	More shots of Captain Fancy's naked behind.
"Home Improvement"	After six seasons the house should be fixed.	Fix the house already.
"The X-Files"	Where is the filing cabinet?	Buy filing cabinet, but never show it. Keeps things suspenseful.
"Monday Night Football"	I'm doing stuff Monday nights.	Move show to Sunday afternoon.

ARE WE OUT THERE?

To: The Big Giant Head

From: Dick Solomon

Re: Us

I have some good news and some bad news. The bad news is:
Humans know about alien existence. The good news is they can't
get enough of us.

We seem to have struck some kind of deep-rooted chord in
their pop culture psyches. Now more than ever, humans are
obsessed and fascinated by the subject of "extraterrestrial
existence" (that's their fancy-schmancy term for us).

Movies portray us as adorable little gremlins or acid-
drooling killing machines. Never research scientists or
accountants. And they often have us out to take over or destroy
the planet. (Like you don't need a permit for something like
that!)

They have television shows, books, T-shirts, video games,
lunch boxes, dolls, and songs about us. The fact is, we're a
billion-dollar industry. And this is the reason for my memo.
I hereby request the chief counsel determine how we can get our
share of the profits. We could use the extra money.

5 Passing Time in Meaningful Ways

S—
"

ere.
local
top
al.

on to win

Really

JL

THE WORKPLACE

One of the big surprises about Earth is the importance of something they call money—green pieces of paper with artwork celebrating dead leaders. (People apparently accept this as barter.) It is essential for survival on this planet; without it, it is impossible to obtain any of the entertainments we've just discussed.

In order to earn this money, you need to work. (I have chosen to work as a physics professor, but there are many other jobs to choose from.) Working exposes you to one of the more fascinating elements of the human experience—the workplace. Although a scary environment at first, it can easily be mastered if you follow a few basic rules on how to handle yourself on the job:

1 Get to know your coworkers. I find the best way to do this is by rifling through their desks and personal belongings.

2 Be friendly to coworkers. A good icebreaker is to ask an officemate his/her salary. Also, I suggest the "pull my finger trick." It is a guaranteed laugh and is sure to make you look witty and intelligent.

3 Never lose sight of the important issues. Office politics and gossip should always be of paramount importance. Don't get sidetracked by work (or you might miss out on something really juicy).

4 No sex in the office. Unless you work in a brothel.

5 Budget your time. Computer games, Xeroxing body parts, and prank e-mail are all well and good, but don't let them get in the way of your lunch hour.

Some Earth jobs require an ornate costume that bestows a great amount of status.

6 Always compliment your underlings. Let them know you appreciate the little people. Remember to talk slowly.

7 Stay clear of work hazards. Never defend a coworker, and always blame your own mistakes on someone else. (Trust me, they're doing it to you.)

8 Constantly challenge your brain. A good exercise to sharpen your language skills is to come up with new things to say to your boss to make him feel important and powerful.

RÉSUMÉ

On this planet, it is important to have a list of all the things you do and/or have done in your life. This way, people can quickly judge you without getting to know you. The following is a copy of what is called my "résumé."

Yet another "challenging" day as professor of astrophysics. Ho-hum.

Dick Solomon
Rutherford, Ohio, Earth, 54335

Experience

Pendelton University
   Extremely well-respected professor of astrophysics.
Responsibilities include:

   —Handing out poor grades to mostly ignorant students.

   —Sharing an office with the lovely Dr. Mary Albright.

   —Trying to instill knowledge into the thick heads of a mostly ignorant class base.

   —Occasionally cleaning Dr. Mary Albright's side of the office to surprise her.

   —Attempting to explain the rather simpleminded theories of astrophysics to students who obviously have very little desire to think.

   —Staring across the office at Dr. Mary Albright as she sits at her desk . . . her bifocals perched precariously on the ridge of her gentle nose as she reads essays with all the delight of a young schoolgirl just blossoming into perky womanhood.

   —Acting as Dr. Mary Albright's knight in shining armor, holding my lance as she watches the sweat glisten on my wrought-iron helmet.

References

   The Big Giant Head
   Dr. Mary Albright
   Mary Albright
   Mary Albright, Ph.D.

GAMES—HOW AND WHEN TO PLAY THEM

There is a human expression: All work and no play makes Jack a dull boy. "Jack" is a famous young boy who went up a hill to fetch a pail of water and met a tragic end in a crown-breaking accident. We can all learn from Jack's sad story; as humans living on Earth, we must play. The following are some games humans have developed:

BOBBING FOR APPLES

Many human games are built around the delightful childhood fantasy of being handicapped: blind (pin the tail on the donkey), Siamese twins (three-legged race), or brain-damaged (boxing). In the bobbing for apples game, a human plays the part of a double amputee whose nourishment has been cruelly tossed into a lake.

TRIVIAL PURSUIT

Humans compete to see whose mind is cluttered with the most pointless facts.

There is time for fun on this planet.

THE PIÑATA

Often played at a child's birthday party. The figure of a cute animal or the child's favorite superhero is hung by the neck from a tree. Delighted at seeing their hero, the children beat him with a stick until he bursts. The children then feast on his candy innards.

BOXING

Two humans hit each other repeatedly until one falls down, preferably unconscious. Fun!

THE CORNISH GAME

Several contestants race to pluck and cook a small hen.

DARTS

Drunk people throw sharp objects in a crowded, dimly lit room.

THREE-CARD MONTE

Simplicity itself. Three cards are displayed facedown. Find the queen and win the green. Your odds of winning are one in three—can't beat that! Though I've had an inexplicable unlucky streak, I've watched with delight as first-timers play and win consistently.

OUTING THE ALIENS AMONG US— A GAME THAT'S "JUST FOR US"

What most humans don't realize is a lot of aliens are already here. Some of them are famous, while others toil in anonymity at the local Dairy Queen dispensing frozen desserts with that perfect curl on top time after time after time after time. Yet no one finds this unusual. Below is a partial list. Some you may have already suspected.

Martha Stewart—No one is that together all the time.

Patrick Swayze—Watch *Roadhouse* for clues.

Nancy Kerrigan—Come on . . . hit with an iron bar and still went on to win a medal? In fact . . .

Almost all professional ice skaters—I mean, look at them. Really look at them.

Deion Sanders—No human could survive an ego that large.

The Jesses—Both Helms and Jackson.

The entire state of Utah—Except for the Osmonds. They are robots.

SPORTS

To fully appreciate the human experience, you must learn to enjoy sports—tests of strength and endurance that usually seem to involve getting balls and putting them somewhere. You should become well versed on the subject, since most people waste a tremendous amount of time talking about sports. Here is a quick guide to some of the more popular sports:

BASEBALL

Nine men try to protect a little ball from nine other men who are intent on hurting it. There is a lot of strategy involved, as well as much crotch-grabbing, butt-slapping, and spitting of dark substances.

FOOTBALL

Also known as basketball and soccer. Men obsessed with balls of various shapes and sizes chase after one another for the right to hold or kick them. More butt-slapping.

GOLF

You drive through a big park in small cars, complaining about how bad you are playing. You stop occasionally to hit a little ball with a long metal stick. Then you complain some more. An extremely dull and laborious game whose object seems to be to stay awake. In my opinion, one of the toughest sports. Even tougher to watch on television. No butt-slapping.

SPECTATING

You and forty-five thousand other people squeeze into a big arena and sit in uncomfortable chairs. For the next several hours, you watch a bunch of men run around a field, all the while drinking a lot of beer, screaming, and yelling out coaching suggestions. Afterward, you fight with one another to see who can find their cars first and exit the arena. This is no easy task, especially if the home team loses. The object appears to be survival. Occasional butt-slapping.

TENNIS

Two players declare their love, then whack a projectile at each other at hundreds of miles an hour. I suggest therapy. No butt-slapping.

PROFESSIONAL WRESTLING

The most exciting of all sports. Two men exhibit amazing feats of strength and bravery. Now that's what I call a real sport! No butt-slapping.

HOBBIES

Humans are fond of saying, "They can put a man on the moon, but I'm bored." That's why they've invented what they call "hobbies."

COLLECTING

Humans enjoy having things. The more of those same things they have, the more they want more of them.

How to Collect Something: Pick something to collect. (Suggestions: postage stamps, those candy dispensers where you break a bird's neck to get the candy, magnets of many nations.) Buy more of them. Then buy more of them. Then buy even more of them. Find more to buy, then do so. Buy some, then buy additional ones. When your collection becomes sufficiently beloved, lock it away in a safe place so it will not be exposed to the damaging effects of light or you. Buy more of whatever it is you are collecting. Eventually, your collection will become very valuable. Don't sell it. When you die, be sure to remind somebody to throw it away.

ANTIQUING

Humans enjoy old things. The older, or more "antique," a thing is, the more valuable humans consider it and the more they want it around. (Exception: people. Old humans are considered to have little value, and nobody wants antique people around. Apparently, the wisdom that comes with age is considered less important than the varnish buildup that comes with age.) As antique furniture is very expensive, some humans choose to artificially distress new furniture by scraping it with a fork or thrashing it with a belt. (Again, this does not work with people.) This way, brand-new furniture can have the decayed, dilapidated look of a real antique in minutes, rather than decades.

SHOOTING THINGS

Humans go out in packs and find animals that are still alive. Then they make them not alive anymore. Through hunting, a human feels the exhilaration that early man felt, going one-on-one against a ferocious adversary who would just as soon kill him—say, a duck or a doe. Laser sights and exploding bullets add to the challenge.

PARACHUTE JUMPING

Humans find it thrilling to jump out of airplanes. Rather than doing this while the plane is on the ground, as any sensible species would do, they wait for the plane to take off. It's not really as dangerous as it sounds—the chances of dying from jumping out of a plane are only ten to fifteen times greater than they are from not jumping out of a plane.

PIERCING

When living as a human, one constant goal is to try to prevent people from putting holes in your body. (This goes hand in hand with Goal #2: Try to keep your blood on the inside.) However, there are some humans who enjoy having extra holes made in their bodies. Rarely do they do anything useful with these holes, such as attaching a permanent key chain. Instead, they adorn them with jewels or rings of precious metal. This says to other humans, "Hey, look at all the extra holes I have!" The chances of infection from a piercing are only ten to fifteen times greater than they are from not having a piercing.

HARRY'S REASONS TO BELIEVE PLANET EARTH HAS A HIGHER POWER

Hummingbirds

Jim Belushi (he still gets work)

Vienetta frozen dessert

Amber Valetta

Tencel fabric (looks like denim, feels like silk)

Kathy Ireland (her waist, it's impossibly long and lean)

Kitchen Bouquet (it turns anything into gravy)

SCHOOL

If humans aren't working or lounging about, chances are they are attending school. Information officer Tommy goes to "high school," where they take bright, inquisitive young humans and turn them into burger-flipping automatons. Following is a sample report he submitted.

BIOLOGY LAB REPORT

MR. VOBURY—THIRD PERIOD

DATE:

NAME: Tommy Solomon

PARTNER: Andy Fore

EXPERIMENT: Dissection of annelid

PURPOSE: To murder an earthworm, look at its organs, and compare them to the perfectly good pictures of dead worms already in the textbook

EQUIPMENT: One filthy cake pan with last year's dried worm juice in it; one rusty scalpel; one probe; one wastebasket to puke in after breathing formaldehyde fumes for an hour.

METHOD: First, worm was selected from a bag. My lab partner Andy confirmed the worm was alive by pretending it was a wiggling strand of snot coming out of his nostril. This was widely confirmed as "funny."
  Then the worm was pinned to the reeking black cake of wax in the pan by plunging pins into its front and rear ends. Then, wielding

the scalpel as a machete, Andy emitted a "kung fu" scream and severed the worm in the middle. A new worm was procured, and we began again.

I made a shallow incision down the center of the worm's body, carefully peeled away the mucousy outer layer of skin, and pinned it down. Its digestive and circulatory organs were exposed. Andy and his football teammates conjectured as to which were the worm's "pecker" and "butt hole."

When Warren Gibson suggested that his worm had larger genitalia than ours, Andy responded by hurling our worm at his head. Warren then used the filthy scalpel to make an incision in Andy's PowerBar. I went back to my desk and copied the diagrams out of the textbook.

RESULTS: Two worms are dead. The science of annelid anatomy has taken a quantum leap forward.

CONCLUSION: It doesn't pay to get a rep as the "smart kid," because lazy Neanderthal mouth-breathers will seek you out as a lab partner.

C-

Your results do not match the results printed in the textbook. Your conclusion does not properly restate the elements of your purpose. You left tweezers out of your equipment. You did not put the date at the top of the page.

TOMMY'S REASONS TO AVOID GYM CLASS

The coach. Being forced to take orders from an insecure, homophobic coach who is trying to vicariously relive his childhood.

Calisthenics. Jumping jacks and running in circles. Am I the only one who sees you do a lot of work and get nowhere?

Basketball. It doesn't do much for your self-esteem to be picked after all the girls.

Baseball, football, soccer, etc. Same reason.

The showers. Smelly and covered in fungus. And that's just the guy next to me.

The locker room. Where wet towels are used as weapons.

Jock straps. Seems to attract ridicule, especially when it's worn over pants.

Sweat. The least appealing of the body's secretions.

Coed gymnastics. Actually, that part's okay.

HOW WELL DO
YOU KNOW EARTH?

Most students are given quizzes, structured much like the one that follows. We recommend giving this quiz to those of us who have been on Earth for a while and think they know their way around. It'll separate the astronauts from the astro*nuts*!

MATCH THE FOLLOWING

1.	Eleanor Roosevelt	A.	Nose-picker
2.	Alexander the Great	B.	Famous inventor
3.	Dwight Eisenhower	C.	Public drunk
4.	Omar Sharif	D.	Egyptian ruin
5.	Merv Griffin	E.	Mind-numbing conversationalist
6.	Darryl Strawberry	F.	Closet homo
7.	Meryl Streep	G.	Meryl Streep
8.	Jonas Salk	H.	Failure
9.	Neil Armstrong	I.	Always late
10.	Stretch Armstrong	J.	Born without a skull
11.	The Fonz	K.	Robot
12.	Joan London	L.	Bed-wetter
13.	Jason Priestley	M.	Could sit on toilet for hours
14.	Margaret Thatcher	N.	Spitter
15.	The girl who played Rhoda	O.	Bit mate on honeymoon

(Answers: We could give you the answers, but what would you have learned? No, better to figure them out for yourself. The best lessons are those you earn.)

HOLIDAYS AND SPECIAL DAYS

If you are going to be staying on Earth for longer than a year, there are certain days you should be aware of. While they are well-intentioned—holidays usually entail taking off from work or school—they are surrounded by frightening customs. It is better to learn about them now than to be caught off guard.

BIRTHDAYS

An annual event to celebrate the day of your birth. Never tell anyone it's your birthday. They will set your food on fire and force you to blow on it. If you are young, an "uncle" may strike you repeatedly from behind for getting older.

VALENTINE'S DAY

On this day, a man will present the object of his affection with a heart-shaped box of chocolates. For some unexplained reason, he may even say, "Life is like a box of chocolates," at which point both the man and loved one will nod knowingly. Although we have only been here briefly, I can say with some authority that life on Earth is not like a box of chocolates. And here is why:

1. There is no lid.

2. If you try to buy life, you will face criminal charges.

3. If you push your thumb into the soft center, it will die.

And why is the heart the symbol of love when the liver is obviously the more attractive organ?

EASTER

Jesus and bunnies. Will someone please explain the connection?

HALLOWEEN

A totally confusing event. Terrifying figures demand payment or they will visit harm on your household.

APRIL 15TH, TAX DAY

Another totally confusing event. Terrifying figures demand payment or they will visit harm on your household.

FUNERALS

People say nice things about you and give you flowers. You even get a ride in the nicest car they can find. But like so many things on Earth, you have to go to the extreme to get attention.

THE DRUID TREE FESTIVAL

(Note: Of all the holidays on Earth, this one is the most important!)

The Druids are a Celtic sect who worship trees. They have been around for well over 2,000 years. Most people in Ohio are Druids.

Although tree worshiping is overt, nearly all humans flatly deny any Druid affiliation. Which leads us to believe that it is an underground cult, much like the Presbyterians.

During the tree-worship season, the midwestern Druid household will bring a tree into the dwelling and decorate it

with ritual ornamentation. Then the family will drive to the nearest enclosed cathedral, like the one on Reynolds Road near the interstate. It is jammed at festival time.

Here, they will purchase offerings for the tree. The offerings are sometimes expensive, but no matter, the spirit of the tree must be fed. The offerings are boxed and wrapped to make them more worthy of the tree.

Then friends and family come by to admire the tree and its bounty. They toast the tree, revel, overeat, and make gaseous noises in its honor. At the peak of the Druid festivities, the offerings are sacrificed.

When the festival is over, the tree is taken out to the curb where it is given a ride in a government vehicle.

The Druid family spends the rest of the year digging its way out of debt, swearing that next season they will not be carried away by the spirit of the tree . . . but they always are.

SOME BASIC RULES

If you are sucked into a human holiday or observance, it will be hard to pull free. You will be expected to join in the celebration like everyone else. Don't panic; just remember that any behavior, no matter how outrageous and strange, is totally acceptable during a holiday. Dancing, singing, barking, howling, breaking wind, and passing out are regular occurrences at many holiday gatherings. These are called "family values."

Here are some things to remember if you are not sure what to do.

1. Drink and eat with abandon. You can't overdo it.

2. Sigh and get sad for no apparent reason.

3. Hug people you barely know and shout, "I love you, man!"

4. Make a toast, forget the words, break down and cry.

5. Laugh way too loud at anecdotes.

6. Make a pass at someone you will have to apologize to later. The more inappropriate, the better.

7. Become pious for at least five minutes.

8. Wear something in the room that shouldn't be worn. (Examples: a lampshade as a hat; a tablecloth as a cape or skirt; a purse as a shoe.)

9. Scream happily if you see someone you didn't expect. The scream should be sudden enough to cause at least two people to spill a beverage.

10. Finally, as you exit, announce loudly, "We should do this more often." Leave and never see them again.

EARTH HUMOR EXPLAINED

One of the human characteristics that is hardest to define is the "sense of humor." Humor is a quality that imbues certain speech and actions; when a human is exposed to these humorous elements, the body spasms involuntarily, producing a "laugh." A laugh is a combination of a hiccup and a scream, sometimes with a hint of oncoming regurgitation. But it is an oddly pleasurable sensation. That is why humans pay other humans to tell humorous stories called "jokes."

What makes a joke funny? Sometimes it is the inappropriate juxtaposition of ideas or the sudden subversion of one's expectations. Sometimes it is the unforeseen crushing of a man's testicles on a bicycle or cactus.

The following are some of the archetypes of Earth humor.

THE POLACK JOKE

QUESTION: How many Polacks does it take to screw in a lightbulb?
ANSWER: Five. One to hold the lightbulb and four to turn the ladder.

This is "funny" on several levels. Firstly, a lightbulb could be screwed in by one regular person, simply by rotating the hand at the wrist. However, because Poland was a communist country whose economy was in shambles, the Poles often had to share a single job between as many as five people, resulting in a ridiculous segmentation of labor. That kind of misery is funny, because it's not yours. Secondly, "lightbulb" is a funny-sounding word, like "pickle" or "sphincter."

THE KNOCK-KNOCK JOKE

JOKESTER: Knock knock.

VICTIM: Who is there?

JOKESTER: Jimmy.

VICTIM: Jimmy who?

JOKESTER: Jimmy Pickle-sphincter.

Here, the humor derives from a surprise. You expect the person to be named Jimmy Owens, or Jimmy Jefferson. But suddenly—*BAM!* Pickle-Sphincter!

THE BAWDY LIMERICK

There once was a man named Dick Solomon
Who was always a perfectly jolly man.
He'd had sex, you see
With Albright, Ph.D.
That handsome young bastard Dick Solomon!

Limericks are funny because the reader is so busy admiring the complex rhyme structure and restrictive metrical form that they don't notice you're being randy until it's too late. Zing!

THE "YOUR MAMA" JOKE

JOKESTER: Your mama is so fat, she uses the rings of Saturn for a girdle!

JOKESTER #2: Oh yeah? Well, *your* mama is so stupid, she thinks Orion's belt is a girdle!

This is funny because typically the combatants don't even know each other's mothers. They are so subsumed in their anger that all they do is lash out with ludicrously ill-informed hypotheses about the mothers' girth, intelligence, hygiene, etc.

THE OBSERVATIONAL JOKE

Have you ever wondered why they call it "throwing up"? Let me tell you, I've vomited, and it doesn't go up. They ought to call it "throwing down."

The observational joker pokes fun at the tiny truisms of daily life—the difficulty humans have opening airline peanuts, the proclivity of elected officials to fib, the high mortality rate of unknown officers on "Star Trek." In so doing, the observational comic makes us laugh . . . but he also makes us think.

THE PIE IN THE FACE

A comic bit of business wherein, in a fit of anger, one person attempts to serve a second person pie. The second person gets the pie all right—everywhere *but* in his mouth! Not an enjoyable way to have pie! The inability of either participant to eat pie makes this both funny and a bit touching.

THE RUBBER CHICKEN

Inedibly hilarious.

THE OLD "SWITCHEROO"

BUFFOONISH MAN: Could you lend me some money?
FUN-LOVING YOUTH: I'd be happy to . . . not!

This is funny because of the clever turn of phrase. Two entire movies were based on this joke! Genius!

FUNNY PEOPLE

There are also many characters who are repeatedly found in comedy movies and television shows. They are funny by their very nature. For instance:

The fat guy

The lady with big breasts

The nearsighted driver

The lusty toreador

The fat dog

The anchorman with no pants

The guy who just won't die

The kid with acne in a plaid shirt

The taxi driver from elsewhere

The scared girl in a bikini

The exasperated rabbi

The man in a gorilla suit

The cursing granny

The cursing British granny

The old man who laughs till he coughs

The nosy bellhop

The ugly horny lady

The coroner eating a sandwich

FUNNY FOODS

Twinkie

Pickle

Bundt cake

Pineapple upside-down cake

Apple pan dowdy

Nilla Wafer

Life cereal

Frosting

Humble pie

Riboflavin

Cake with a file in it

Poisonous mushroom

PRACTICAL JOKES: NOT JUST PRACTICAL—FUN, TOO!

One good way to become friends with a human is to embarrass him in front of his friends and coworkers. That's what makes these jokes practical. Here are some suggestions for jokes you can do.

YES, WE HAVE BANANAS! Make friends with someone who enjoys bananas. Buy hundreds of bananas at a store. Then ask your friend if he wants any bananas. When he says "yes," give him the hundreds of bananas you have bought. No matter how much he enjoys bananas, this is probably more than he was expecting. Respond, "You said you wanted bananas!" (This practical joke will also work with apricots. Simply substitute apricots for bananas and voilà!)

DEATH IN THE FAMILY Tell a friend there's been a death in his family, perhaps a spouse or parent. After the crying jag, tell him you were "just kidding." Boy, will his face be red!

FAKE CAR WRECK JOKE Make friends with somebody who's just bought a brand-new car. Ask to borrow his car. Have him say "yes." Smash in the front of his car with a sledgehammer or rock. When he sees the car, tell him you were in a terrible car wreck. He will be horrified! Then tell him what *really* happened. Enjoy the good joke.

COCKROACH BURGER   Invite your friend over for burgers, but don't say what kind of burger you will be serving. Make your burger out of traditional ground beef. Make his burger out of cockroaches. (Note: Be sure to remember which is which.) If he complains that his burger tastes "funny," tell him it's a new recipe that everybody's talking about. (Note: Try not to laugh when you say this. It will lessen the effectiveness of the joke.) After he's finished eating the burger, ask him, "How did you like your cockroach burger? That's right, I said 'cockroach burger.' As in 'a burger made of cockroaches.'" No wonder it tasted funny!

THE ART OF ARGUMENT

The locals love to argue. And they'll argue about anything: brown vs. brunette, basketball vs. football, Roe vs. Wade. When you see an argument starting, remember: Jump right in! They'll be insulted if you don't. It doesn't even matter if you know anything about the subject being argued. In fact, it's helpful if you don't. That way, you can argue with abandon without being distracted by what your point is. Yet, even though arguing is so common, most people are deficient in its art, finding it impossible to persuade others into believing what they believe. It is, of course, one of the easiest things to do. Here are some secrets.

KEEP SAYING: "YOU'RE WRONG"

These are two simple, monosyllabic words, but you wouldn't believe how many people forget to use them during an argument. Just keep saying, "You're wrong," or "Nope, you're wrong," or "You are absolutely wrong, mister" throughout the argument. Sometimes, the act of persuasion can be done with the most unpretentious discussion.

ALWAYS LAUGH IN THE PERSON'S FACE

Not only will the other person become increasingly agitated when laughed at, and often give up, but it releases a great deal of tension in you, the "laugher." Use laughter about three minutes into the argument, preferably during the other person's most heated moment. If they ask what you're laughing at say: "You, silly. But go on."

USE PRINCIPLES OF LOGIC

If the person you're arguing with makes a statement, always use that statement against that person. For example, the person says, "Pumpernickel bread tastes good." After saying, "You're wrong" and "Nope, mister, you're wrong," then laughing, start using principles of logic. In this case, you might say: "Consider the transitive theory? If A equals B and B equals C, then A equals C." The person will be momentarily confused, until you explain: "If you like pumpernickel bread, and I don't like pumpernickel bread, and you don't like me, that means you don't like pumpernickel bread." The person's argument will instantly fall apart, making victory yours.

TURN AND RUN AWAY

If the person hasn't given up by this point, turn and run away. The person will realize that anyone who has the guts to actually run as far as he can in the other direction is probably right. "Why else would he run?" the person will ask himself. And then the person will say, "Damn it. I'm wrong again."

Follow these four simple lessons and arguments will always lead to a clear winner. You. (Or me . . . if that's who you happen to be arguing with.)

My powers of persuasion
obviously have the
mismatched
Mrs. Dubcek reeling.

6 Words, Wisdom, and Katie Katie Katie!

age
el,
mon,
nder

b,
lle

s
rather
, "Why
hmael a
ndered
asterful
five dol-

hat his
as the
. And
lle
? Or

rning
ting
Ohio.
rence
l see,
ed, as
ain,"

his

THE WRITTEN WORD

A wise man once said, "The spoken word isn't worth the paper it's written on." I don't know what he meant, but I can tell you this: Books sell for up to $26.95 a pop. And that makes writing an art form.

The written word falls into four categories: poetry, prose, fiction, and graffiti. I intended to provide you with an example of fiction, but copyright law makes that prohibitively expensive. So instead, I will give you a sneak preview of my own work-in-progress, the "great Earth novel." It is admittedly just a rough draft, but, at the risk of sounding immodest, it is wonderful.

Author! Author!

Chapter One

"Call me, Ishmael."

"I'll try," Ishmael replied. "I'll be busy with my job, teaching physics to a ragtag bunch of students at Centerville University who look up to me as a hero."

Dr. Ishmael Van Parkingham felt her eyes burning holes into his back as he turned to leave. Not literally, but rather in the sense that she was staring after him, thinking, "Why isn't a man as handsome and fiercely intelligent as Ishmael a world leader?" Why indeed? Every woman who met him wondered the same thing, even those he hadn't just had long, masterful sex with, which left them both spent like yesterday's five-dollar bill.

But Ishmael had bigger fish to fry, in the sense that his students were, figuratively speaking, fish, and frying was the act of trying to turn their lives around with learning. And there ahead of him was the frying pan itself: Centerville University. Could he get through to his students today? Or would this day be a fish fry of futility?

The day, by the way, was hot, the September Sun burning in the sky like a flaming pie, its orange intensity blasting the parched godforsaken landscape that was Centerville, Ohio. The Sun mocked Ishmael, saying, "You can't make a difference in these kids' lives," but in a mocking voice. "We shall see, Mr. Sun. We shall see." A few hollow-eyed students stared, as if to say, "Dr. Van Parkingham is talking to the Sun again," but they dared not. Dr. Ishmael Van Parkingham was the strongest man in town, and not afraid to prove it. With his fists. In a fight situation.

(TO BE CONTINUED!!!!)

SALLY ON WOMEN'S PUBLICATIONS

On this planet, women are considered vastly inferior to men intellectually. For this reason, women have their own special literature. Literature that also caters to their impulsiveness, insecurity, self-loathing, and desire to be led. These are called "magazines for women" or "women's magazines."

There is a large selection to choose from. You can select the one most suitable for you (if you're a woman) by scanning the glossy covers. The contents of the magazines are printed in provocative sound bites like:

"Bigger Breasts on a Budget"

"The Hour-Long Orgasm"

"Are You a Closet Binger?"

"When to Stop Hating Your Mother"

"Fighting Yeast Forever"

"The New Leg"

"Computers Made Glamorous"

"Bigger Breasts on a Budget"

"How to Tell if You're Happy"

"Fall's New Slenderizing Hats"

"The New Eye"

"How to Make Boring Sex Tolerable"

"Bigger Breasts on a Budget"

Popular Magazines for Women

Elle — For younger women with a lot of time and a lot of money who like articles about movie stars and singers.

Glamour — For even younger women with less money but still a lot of time who like articles about saving time.

Seventeen — For girls who have nothing but time. And pimples.

Mirabella — For older women who wish they were younger who have a lot of money but don't have a lot of time and like articles about money.

My favorite women's magazine is *Cosmopolitan*, because in every issue they include a quiz or test for you to take. I commend the publishers on trying to keep us gals sharp and alert. So if you're ready to do some thinkin', get a *Cosmo*.

Attached is my version of a *Cosmo* quiz that you can practice on.

While I read a "women's magazine," Sally checks to make sure that my head has indeed become empty.

SALLY'S *COSMO* QUIZ

1. You meet a man who is attractive. What do you do to get his attention?

  A. Act demure and helpless.

  B. Shoot him in the neck with a tranquilizer dart and drag him back to your place.

  C. Point out that his broad neck and thick shoulders make you feel he would be an agile hunter who would provide well for your children.

2. Which of the following books appeals to you?

  A. *Women Who Love Too Much.*

  B. *Women Who Run with the Wolves.*

  C. *Women Who Don't Get Why the Men in This Mission Complain.* If they just once had to go through what I have to go through to get ready in the morning, or faced the problem of water retention, not to mention the fact that nobody, and I mean nobody, can buy off the rack. And who said women have to change styles every year for no reason at all, and if I find the guy who invented the underwire bra, he is a dead man. . . . I'm sorry, forgot the question.

3. When a woman at the makeup counter asks you if you are familiar with "their system," you should reply . . .

  A. "Yes, I'm familiar with your system. It's nine planets and a yellow star."

  B. "Yes, but if I wanted to be that painted, I would have gone to Earl Schieb."

  C. "I'm just looking, and I don't like what I see!"

4. After a very hot date, he says he'll call you. He never does. You should . . .

  A. Realize that this is a line men use without thinking.

  B. Forget about any man who says one thing and does another.

  C. Kick his door in and check his phone.

5. You can easily get any man to commit to you with . . .

  A. A night of incredible sex.

  B. A sincere and honest exchange of ideas.

  C. An incredible night of sex.

6. You are having an argument with a man at a party. He says he can "change your little mind" about things. You should . . .

  A. Ignore his rude comment.

  B. Show your displeasure and walk away.

  C. Offer to "change his mind" by taking it out of his skull and putting it in the punch bowl.

7. You will be unforgettable in bed if you . . .

  A. Kiss great.

  B. Move like he's paying for it.

  C. Bite, spit, kick, and yell.

To: Big Giant Head
From: Harry Solomon
Re: Katie Couric Biography

cc: Katie Couric, Dick, Bryant Gumbel, Al Roker, and Matt Lauer

She's a tiny waif with a bob haircut and a face full of teeth that sparkle under the hot TV lights like shiny pebbles sparkling under hot TV lights. Her name is Katie Couric, the co-owner of the "Today" show, and she has the same effect on me as does Pez candy. I just can't get enough (although Katie has no dispenser). Here's a glimpse into Katie's life ... a life filled with happy days, bubble baths, puppy dogs, and Manhattan-style clam chowder.

THE UNAUTHORIZED BIOGRAPHY OF KATIE COURIC
by Harry Solomon

When I think of Katie Couric, two words come to mind: Katie Couric. Say it soft and there's music playing. Say it loud and it sounds like something beautiful is caught in your throat. Katie Couric is, as we all know, the most beautiful of all the humans on the "Today" show. But what you may not know is that most of what she says on TV is directed at me.

Katie Couric's entire twenty-four years of life have been spent hosting the "Today" show. I've never seen her do anything else. I've heard rumors that she occasionally does guest spots on "Dateline NBC," but there's no way to verify that. Katie Couric lives, breathes, eats, digests, and regurgitates the "Today" show.

She's as cute as a mutton and she cares. For example, she genuinely seems upset when the person at the news desk reports some bad news. It's like she's thinking to herself: "Boy, that was some bad news," or "That news was not good at all." She's not thinking to herself: "How is my hair?" or "Do I look cute?" I get the feeling Bryant frequently has those thoughts. I also like the way she laughs at the fat guy who does the weather. And it doesn't matter which fat guy. She always laughs. And he's always fat. I remember once he said something about "the dew point," which sounded dirty.

And who on television has more integrity than Katie Couric? For example, when Katie says, "We'll be right back," she means "We'll be right back." Not in ten years, not in twenty minutes. And not just back. Right back. After those long dreadful commercials that keep me from my true love. And I guarantee, if she didn't come right back, she'd throw a fit: "Why aren't we right back?" she'd yell. "I said I'd be right back and damn it, I want to be right back!" "But Katie," they'd argue, "nuclear weapons have been deployed by the enemy and are going to land in New York within the hour! We have to cut away to a special report!" But this just angers my fiery little vixen: "Special report, my butt! I've got a special report about a Minnesota dairy farmer whose cow is best friends with his dog!" "But, Katie—the missiles!" "Screw the missiles! I want the cow!" And sure enough, there would be Katie. Right back. With the cow.

Katie also does the best interviews on TV. Sure, there are other interviewers: Barbara Walters, the old men on "60 Minutes," and Conan. They're all okay. But they all have one thing going against them: They're not Katie Couric. Katie makes her guests feel comfortable, like she's talking to an old friend in some living room in some cabin somewhere, after a long day of hiking on some mountain where they found some rock that they lost and then spent the rest of the day looking for until it got dark, and they gave up and went back to the cabin, totally exhausted. Then Katie asked her friend if she could do an interview. And that's where we tune in. Except they never talk about the rock. It's always about a book or a movie. One of these days, I'd like to hear about that rock. And one of these days, I will.

Katie has a husband. But I don't hold that against her. How was she supposed to know I was coming to Earth? I don't know her husband's name, but who the heck cares? We're talking about Katie here, not her stupid husband. She also has a couple of kids—the luckiest children in the history of this planet (including Richie Rich). Oh, to call Katie Couric "mom."

Katie is a jack-of-all-trades. I've seen her cook a pasta primavera, with just a touch of saffron oil to bring out the taste in the rigatoni. I've seen her exercise with Dr. Art Ulene (what kind of name is that for a doctor?), bending her knees and swinging her arms during pregnancy. I've seen her put together a beautiful Easter basket with "flowers you can cut from your own garden," including weeds. ("Weeds?" she asked.) She's cut and pasted homemade chintz. Stood outside in the cold. Got in one of those weightless machines. Rode a roller coaster. Petted a giraffe. Taken a dance lesson. Sung a Christmas carol. Eaten a variety of brownies, with and without nuts.

I will conclude with a poem about Kate Couric. It's called "A Poem About Katie Couric." And it goes something like this:

A POEM ABOUT KATIE COURIC

The todays of the "Today" show turn into yesterdays
>   When tomorrow's today comes.
But Katie is always there, making "Today" today
>   Without thought of tomorrow's "Today" or yesterday's "Today."
Katie is always in today's "Today."
>   And that is why today is always so special.

>   I wrote that.

SUBJECT

Words You Can Make out of the Letters in Katie Couric's Name

DATA

Katie	Tack	Route	Trice	Ice
Couric	Rack	Rout	Taker	Icer
Katiecouric	Sick	Catiekouric	Cater	Rue
Cat	Court	Tire	Tear	Rote
Tour	Trek	Take	Route	Irate
Tie	Trick	Rice	Our	Rate

SUBJECT

Some Words You Can't Make out of the Letters in Katie Couric's Name

DATA

Bazooka	Stinky	Shrapnel	Please	Collapsing
Korea	Who	Vietnam	Call	Help
Gorilla	Chimp	Horrible	Have	Cannot
Bryantgumbel	Wall	Tragedy	No	Stand
Schedule	Three	Tears	Friends	Up

TWO MORE POEMS by HARRY

ODE TO A BOILED HOT DOG ONE FOOT LONG

There you are, my boiled friend.

You are very beautiful sitting on my plate.

Is there something on your mind?

You seem unusually quiet this evening.

Yes, I have overheard your conversations with the authorities.

Did you actually think you could fool me?

And now, ready the sauerkraut, and let the meal begin!

I SAW A MOUSE EATING A PIECE OF CHEESE

I saw a mouse eating a piece of cheese.

It was wearing a blue suit and wing-tip shoes.

It was speaking on a cellular phone.

It drove a new car.

You've guessed it, haven't you?

The mouse is *YOU!!*

HAIKU

Five short syllables

Follow with a line of seven

Then: Another five.

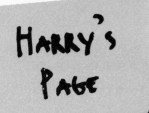

WHERE'S WHERE'S WALDO

Humans are constantly on the lookout for things that waste their lives away. Whether it's daydreaming, writing interoffice memos, or watching VH1, humans will forever find ways to drain the life out of each precious hour they live.

One of these pastimes is a series of popular books called *Where's Waldo*. Waldo, a tall, bespectacled young man with a red-and-white-striped cap, is supposedly hidden in various supposedly intricate pictures throughout the book. The object is simple: Find Waldo. Why anybody would take the time to look for Waldo in the first place astounds me. When you find him, you don't get a prize. You don't even get the satisfaction of saying how much better you are than everybody else (like at the Olympics). All you get do is say, "There he is." And that just doesn't seem worth it.

However, the original book—*Where's Waldo*—is so popular, I thought it behooved me to tell you where he was, just in case someone asked.

PICTURE ONE. Directly above the man handing girlfriend flowers at the bottom of the right-hand page.

PICTURE TWO. Three people over from the blue-and-white umbrella, which is just to the right the large postcard on the top of the left-hand page.

PICTURE THREE. Next to the skiing snowman above the ice rink, near the bottom of the right-hand page.

PICTURE FOUR. Next to the "hippie tent" near the bottom of the right-hand page.

PICTURE FIVE. Under Waldo's signature on the large postcard at the top of the left-hand page.

PICTURE SIX. Above the squirting fire truck in the center of the right-hand page.

PICTURE SEVEN. Three inches from the top. Four inches from the right. On the right-hand page.

PICTURE EIGHT. To the right of the two confused security guards wearing green clothes above the dinosaur's head on the left-hand page.

PICTURE NINE. Standing on the boat, next to the guy about to vomit in the ocean, near the bottom of the right-hand page.

PICTURE TEN. To the left of the three bears at the picnic table, near the top of the right-hand page.

PICTURE ELEVEN. Four people down from where the woman is getting her clothes vacuumed off, on the top right side of the right-hand page.

PICTURE TWELVE. One person down from the little girl who's standing under the weight lifter's weights that are about to crush her to death in the middle of the left-hand page.

Enjoy!

EARTH WISDOM

Earthlings, on the whole, are not a particularly intelligent species. (With their small brains, it's amazing they ever made it out of the cave.) Be that as it may, they have, on rare occasion, come up with a catchy phrase or two that imparts some bit of advice. Here are a few of their words of wisdom.

Thou shalt not kill. (Short, simple, and to the point. An interesting idea, in theory.)

I think, therefore I am. (A bold statement that wisely dismisses three-quarters of the planet's population.)

Beauty is only skin deep. (This one's a fact. You wouldn't believe how ugly they are on the inside.)

You can't teach an old dog new tricks. (If you did, what would the new dogs do?)

Money can't buy you happiness. (It can only buy things that will make you happy.)

You get what you pay for. (Really good advice, considering what happens when you try to get what you didn't pay for.)

Don't look a gift horse in the mouth. (Horse saliva stings.)

To err is human. (At least they admit it.)

All's fair in love and war. (Although hand grenades are generally appropriate only for the latter.)

An apple a day keeps the doctor away. (Imparts the benefits of a strong arm and well-aimed fruit.)

If the shoe fits, wear it. (Always wear comfortable and correctly sized footwear.)

Crime doesn't pay. (Which is why it's a good thing you can trade in the things you stole for money.)

Don't leave home without it. ("It" is pants.)

You can't take it with you. (Unless it's pants.)

Money can't buy you love. (This isn't just good advice. It's the law.)

Just do it. (A bit vague, but wise nonetheless.)

A penny saved is a penny earned. (Good point, but makes more sense with larger denominations.)

There's a lot of fish in the sea. (133, 756,329,644 of them.)

7 The End

a

p

n.

everyone

alth of

th.

sh.

ead. I

has

way.

iverse

actual

EARTH: GOOD AND BAD

GOOD THINGS ABOUT EARTH

General roundness.

Bikini capital of the Universe.

Heartburn medicines now available without prescription.

Pleasant to the touch.

The innocence of a small child.

Nougat.

Human tongues generally hairless.

Cast of "Melrose Place" will eventually die.

BAD THINGS ABOUT EARTH

Sometimes Chex Mix has peanuts, sometimes not. What's the deal?

How many "Star Trek" shows are there, anyway?

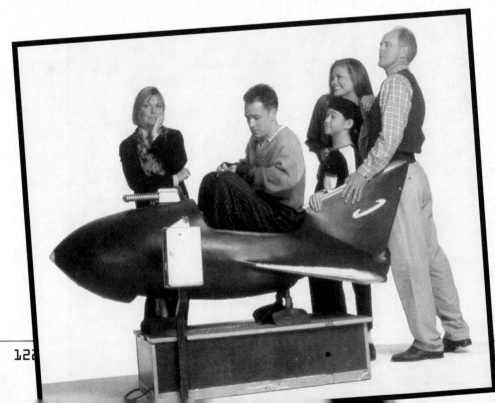

Intolerance.

Cast of "Melrose Place" still alive for now.

No running in pool areas.

Rules for retransmitting professional basketball games are so restrictive it's a joke.

Surround sound is prohibitively expensive.

Video stores never have the movie you want.

Those little network logos in the corner of your television screen.

French people think they're so great; they're just little people on a small blot of land on a tiny planet.

DICK: THINGS I'M TAKING BACK WITH ME

As baggage room will be limited on the trip home, I've carefully come up with a list of things that I will be bringing back with me after the mission.

The Bible. The original rule book.

Balloons. Gift-wrapped bags of Earth's atmosphere. For everyone back home.

The National Enquirer. So we can get updates on the health of the potato baby.

Michael Bolton. Our farewell gesture of gratitude to Earth.

Grape Nyquil. Bold and impertinent, it goes great with fish.

Giant foam "We're #1" hand. A gift for the Big Giant Head. I know it's stupid, but what do you get for the Head who has everything?

The Moon. We'll pick that up when we leave. It's on the way.

Windows 95. We don't want to be the only guys in the Universe without it. And some of it actually works.

Cherry-red 1964 Rambler. Since I can't bring back my actual penis.

A lock of Mary's hair, one of Mary's shoes, a scraping of cells from . . . Oh, who am I kidding? I need the whole Mary! She'll ride up front with me.

SALLY:
THINGS I'M TAKING BACK

Three pairs size 8 Manolo Blahnik stacked-heel slingbacks. I'm not leaving Earth without them.

A tampon. Oh, the memories.

Jimmy Smits's butt.

Chanels 1, 5, and 22.

Eight-ounce bottle of Pert. Shampoo and conditioner in one!

Revlon "Passionate Plum" lipstick. Because it goes with everything.

Age-defying makeup.

Gravity-defying bra.

HARRY:
THINGS I'M TAKING BACK

Katie Couric. I know we're not supposed to abduct humans, but she's so cute and cuddly, how can I resist?

A million dollars.

Earmuffs. Actually, we don't have ears, so I guess I'll have to take some of those, too.

A barrel of monkeys. What could be more fun?

Styrofoam peanuts. Covered in bubble wrap for protection.

A beautiful sunset on the beach. As soon as I figure out how.

Me.

TOMMY:
THINGS I'M TAKING BACK

Coach Strickland's whistle. An example of a primitive yet effective weapon of torture.

***Playboy*'s "Girls of the Pac Ten" special double issue.** It's got some really good articles. And hey, it's a long ride back.

Billy Klausner's skateboard. It's not that I'm any good at it, I just want that jerk looking for it for the rest of his life.

A friendship bracelet. August would kill me if I ever took it off.

Another *Playboy* magazine.

Mystery meat–day lunch. I want to have it analyzed by the guys in the lab.

***Penthouse* magazine.**

INDEX

Quotes,
    mine, 45–80, 81–103,
        104
    somebody else's, (TBA)

Rabbits, 29–31
Rasputin, Grigory, 229
Rats, 479
Reality, 22
    why it's overrated, 388
Reentry, 141
Rejection, 266
Rest, need for, 367
Reverie, state of, 83
Revulsion, periods of, 274
Rivets, 234–59
    connection to frogs,
        255
    fascinating history of,
        234–34 1/2
Row, row, row your boat, 883
Solomon, King, 11
Solomon
    High Commander Dick,
        1–2349

dashing qualities of,
    66–87
intellect of, 34–59
sexual conquests of,
    99–785
Sally, Harry, Tommy,
    here and there
    (you'll find them,
    I'm sure)
Nothing else of importance in
    the world of S's

Tacos, 442
Taoism, 214
Teutonic women, 55
    why Tommy loves 'em,
        56–107
Textured vegetable protein, 57
Tomatoes, fresh
    baked bulgur-stuffed,
        146–47
    crushing them against
        your forehead, 133
    peeling and seeding of,
        127
Tortoises, 127–28

Trees, 9–11, 47, 52, 58–59
    dancing and, 56
    residing under, 57
    sap of, 48
    thoughts of, 90

U, V, W, X: The most boring
    letters in the alphabet. I
    refuse to index them.

Yahoo, 367
Yodeling, 784
    art of, 787
    preventing avalanches,
        792
    without sounding like a
        girl, 788
Yoohoo, 189

Zander, Christine,
    Andy of, 32, 45–46
Zoo,
    Andy of, 44
    Bronx, 34
    Morning, 97

Market Research Survey

Fellow aliens, thank you for purchasing *The Official Report on Earth,* by High Commander Dick Solomon. So that we might better serve you in the future, please take a brief moment to answer the following questions. All answers will be sent directly to the Big Giant Head for processing.

1. How did you hear about this book? (Check all that apply.)

__Advertising	__Coworker	__Processing drone
__Store display	__Tattooed woman	__Word of mouth
__Friend	__Casual acquaintance	__Friend of friend
__Ex-spouse	__This guy I know	__This other guy

2. What made you purchase this book? (Check all that apply.)

__Looked good	__Promise of nudity	__Ordered at gunpoint
__Black text on white background	__Large inheritance	__This guy I know
__Hefty price tag	__Impress my friends	__Impress this guy I know

3. How old are you? (Check all that apply.)

__Under 20	__20–21	__22–47
__48–48 ½	__48 ½–80	__Over 80
__Over 81	__Over 90	__Other

4. What other books have you recently purchased?

__*Don't Shoot, It's Only Me,* by Bob Hope

__Other

5. Which leisure activities do you enjoy on a regular basis? (Check all that apply.)

__Running	__Sailing	__Alcohol abuse
__Sitting	__Standing	__Zoo-going
__Self-immolation	__Sex (one partner)	__Sex (many partners)

6. What is your yearly income?

__A lot	__Some	__Not very much

7. If you could change the amount of money you make, would you like to make:

__More money

__Less money

__Same amount of money as now

__Don't know/NA

8. Are you a woman?

__Yes	__No

(*If "no," go on to Question 9.*)

    8a. Are you beautiful?

__Yes	__No

    8b. Would you consider going out with me?

__Yes	__No

9. If you could control the weather, would you like it to be:

   __More sunny   __More rainy   __Partly cloudy

   __Freezing rain   __Melting snow   __Don't know/NA

10. On average, how many books do you buy in one month?

   __100   __More than 100

11. What do you look for in microwavable foods? (Check all that apply.)

   __Delicious taste   __Convenience   __General lack of poison

   __Food that awakens   __Extremely valuable   __Corn

      magical powers   jewel in every fifth box   __Other

12. If you could be any kind of tree, what kind would it be?

   __Oak

   __Maple

   __Some crazy other kind of tree

13. If you could order anybody dead without fear of retribution, who would it be?

_____

Address_____

Please rate the following on a scale of 1 to 5 (1 = extremely unsatisfactory; 2 = somewhat unsatisfactory; 3 = mildly satisfactory; 4 = terrific; 5 = extremely satisfactory). Be sure to circle your answer with a #2 pencil. If you want to change your answer, please buy a fresh copy of this book.

Content of this book	1	2	3	4	5
Content of *Don't Shoot, It's Only Me*, by Bob Hope	1	2	3	4	5
Amount of nudity	1	2	3	4	5
Quality of nudity	1	2	3	4	5
Limited Edition gold-leaf cover (if applicable)	1	2	3	4	5
The health-care crisis	1	2	3	4	5
Judd Hirsch's performance in *Independence Day*	1	2	3	4	5
No really, he was a caricature, right?	1	2	3	4	5

The following information is for statistical purposes only. It will be used by the Big Giant Head to determine your suitability for continued existence.

Name _____
       (last, first, middle initial, first, last)

Political Affiliation _____

Greatest Fear _____

Ethnic Group You Most Hate _____

Most Damaging Secret _____

The Big Giant Head appreciates your help.

The Big Giant Head
Never too big or giant to care.

ACKNOWLEDGMENTS

SPECIAL THANKS TO:

Marcy Carsey, Tom Werner, Caryn Mandabach, Peter Torotorici, Stuart Glickman, Courtney Conte, David Tochterman, Patrick Kienlen, Time Ryder, Gil Goldberg, Katy Ballard, James Anderson, Garvin Eddy, Melina Root, Mauro DiPreta, Joni Evans, John, Jane, Kristen, French, Joey, Simbi, and Elmarie.

AND THANKS TO:

Bob Berlinger, Jim Burrows, Marc Hirschfeld, Michael Katcher, SVC Television London, Don Ohlmeyer, Warren Littlefield, Jamie Tarses, Karey Burke, Flody Suarez, Stu Bloomberg, Kim Fleary, Carolyn Ginsburg, Vince Humphrey, Ben Vaughn, Jayne Kehoe, Johnny Foam, Tara Stephenson, Cliff Bernay, Ashley Davies, Ron Browne, the entire crew on Stage 15 Radford, Bunny Dinsmore, and American Motors.